COPYRIGHT 2020 BY TOLEN MEDIA

ALL RIGHTS RESERVED.

THIS BOOK OR ANY PORTION THEREOF MAY NOT BE REPRODUCED OR USED IN ANY MANNER WHATSOEVER WITHOUT THE EXPRESS WRITTEN PERMISSION OF THE PUBLISHER EXCEPT FOR THE USE OF BRIEF QUOTATIONS IN A BOOK REVIEW.

PRINTED IN THE UNITED STATES OF AMERICA
ISBN: 9798603620497
FIRST PRINTING, 2020

Color My Visions Series
@TOLENMEDIA (INSTAGRAM/FACEBOOK)

TOLENMEDIA@GMAIL.COM
WWW.TOLEN.MEDIA

Dedication

For my oldest brother, Marcus Deshay...the first person to inspire my art mind and make me think being able to draw what you see is a very cool talent to be born with. He drew me the best picture ever of Michael Jordan dunking and sent it to me at one of the lowest times in my life and I'll never forget showing it off, saying "my brother drew that!"

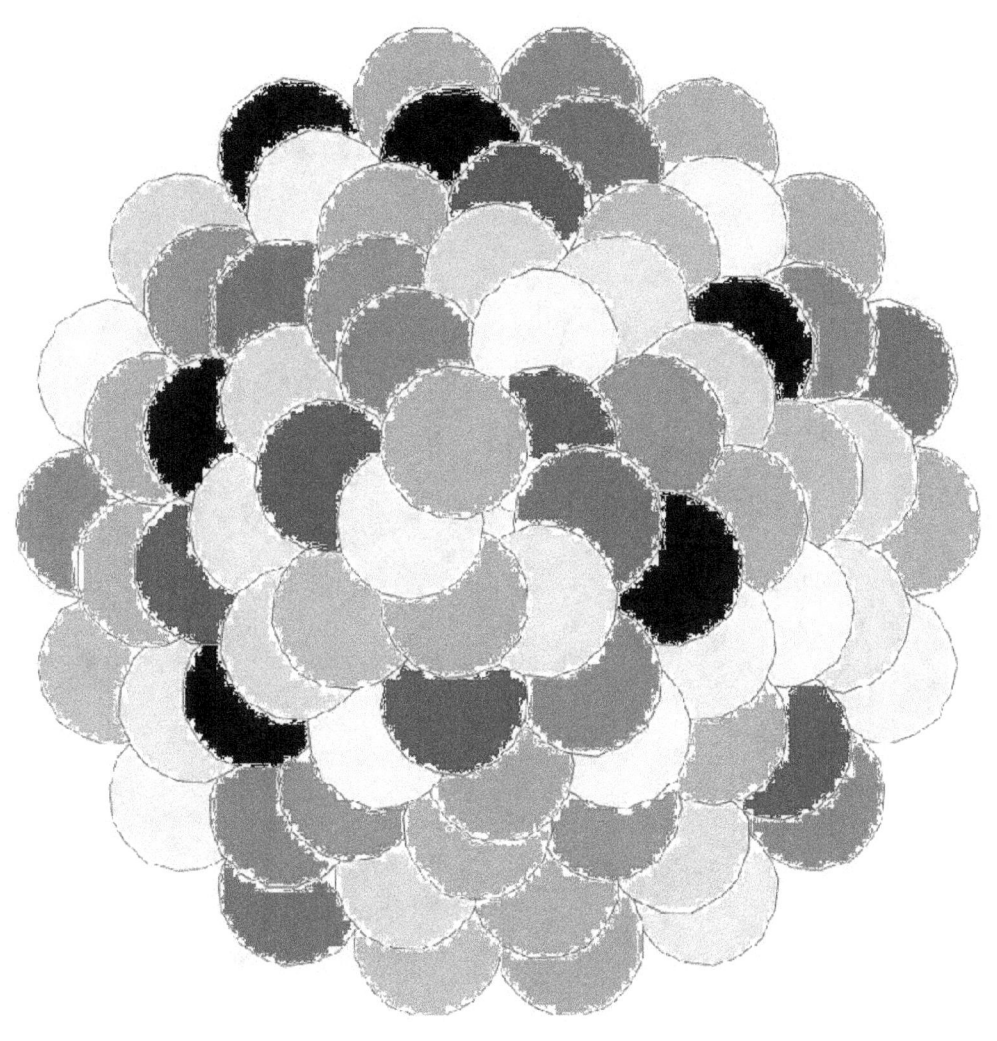

AND I COLOR

Get out your rainbow colors and make today beautiful!

A Color My Visions® series adult coloring book by Christopher Conrad

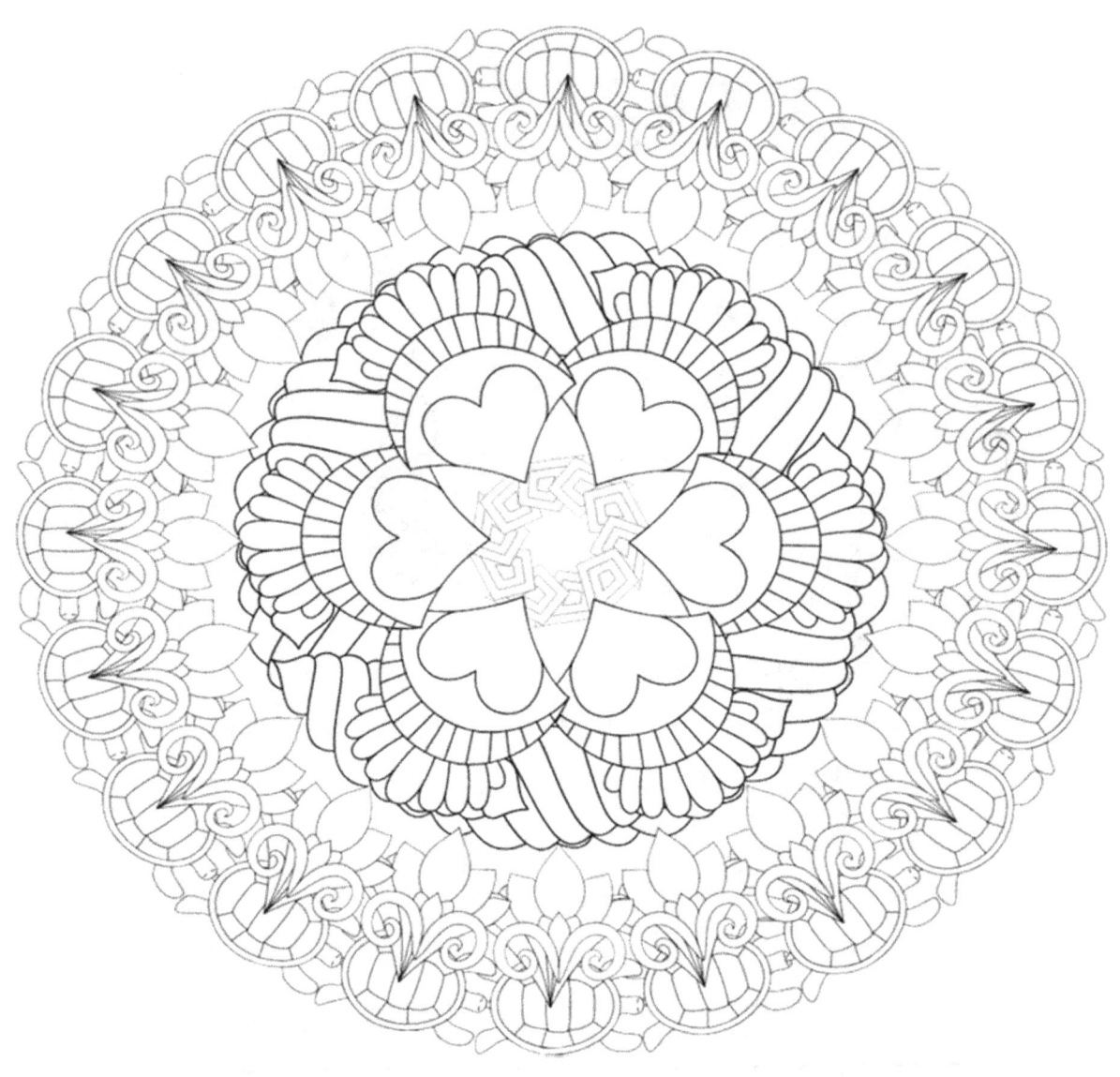

"Of all God's gifts to the sighted man, color is holiest, the most divine, the most solemn."
– John Ruskin

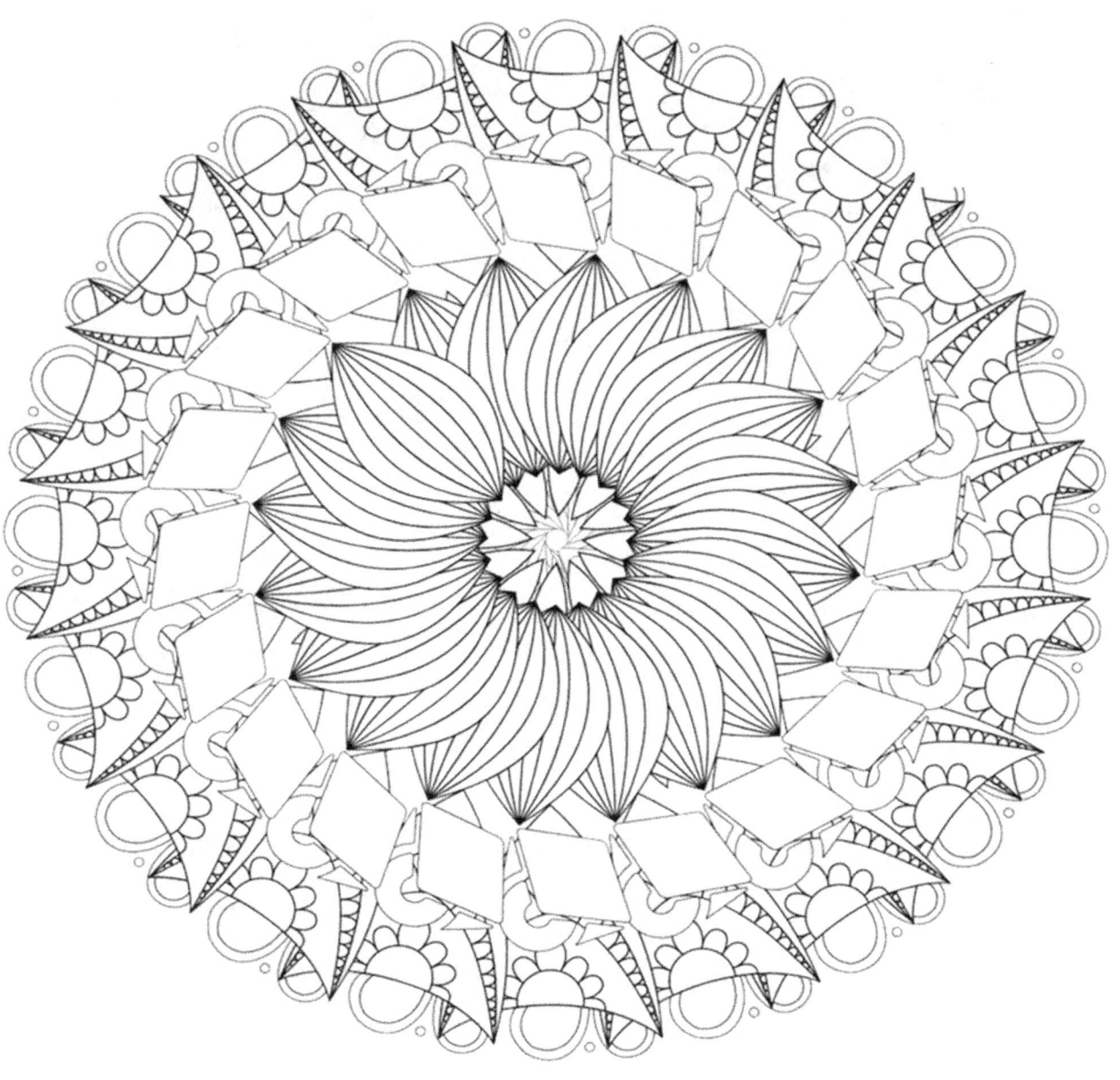

"In nature, light creates the color.
In the picture, color creates the light."
– Hans Hofmann

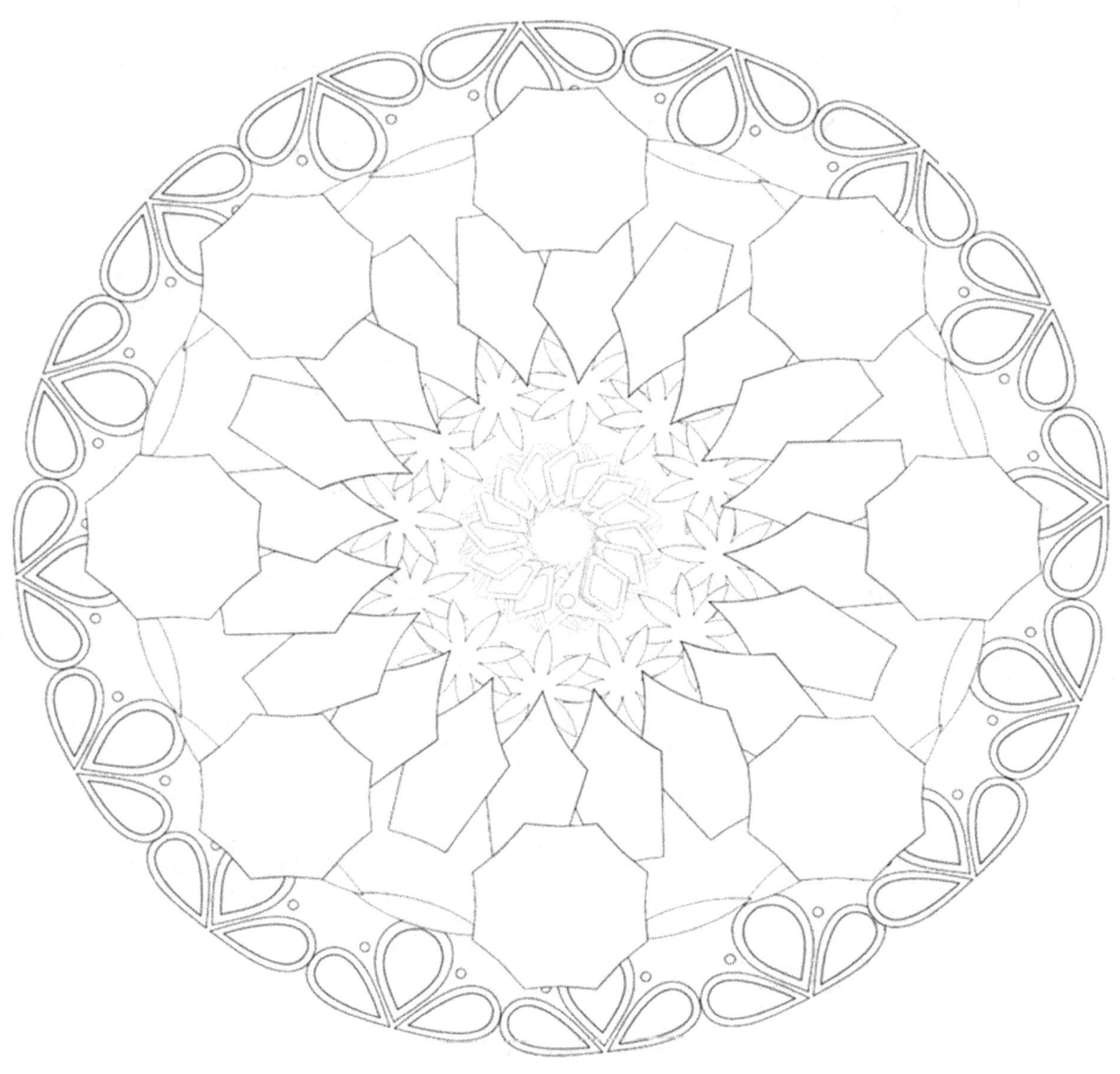

"Light is a thing that cannot be reproduced, but must be represented by something else – by color."
– Paul Cezanne

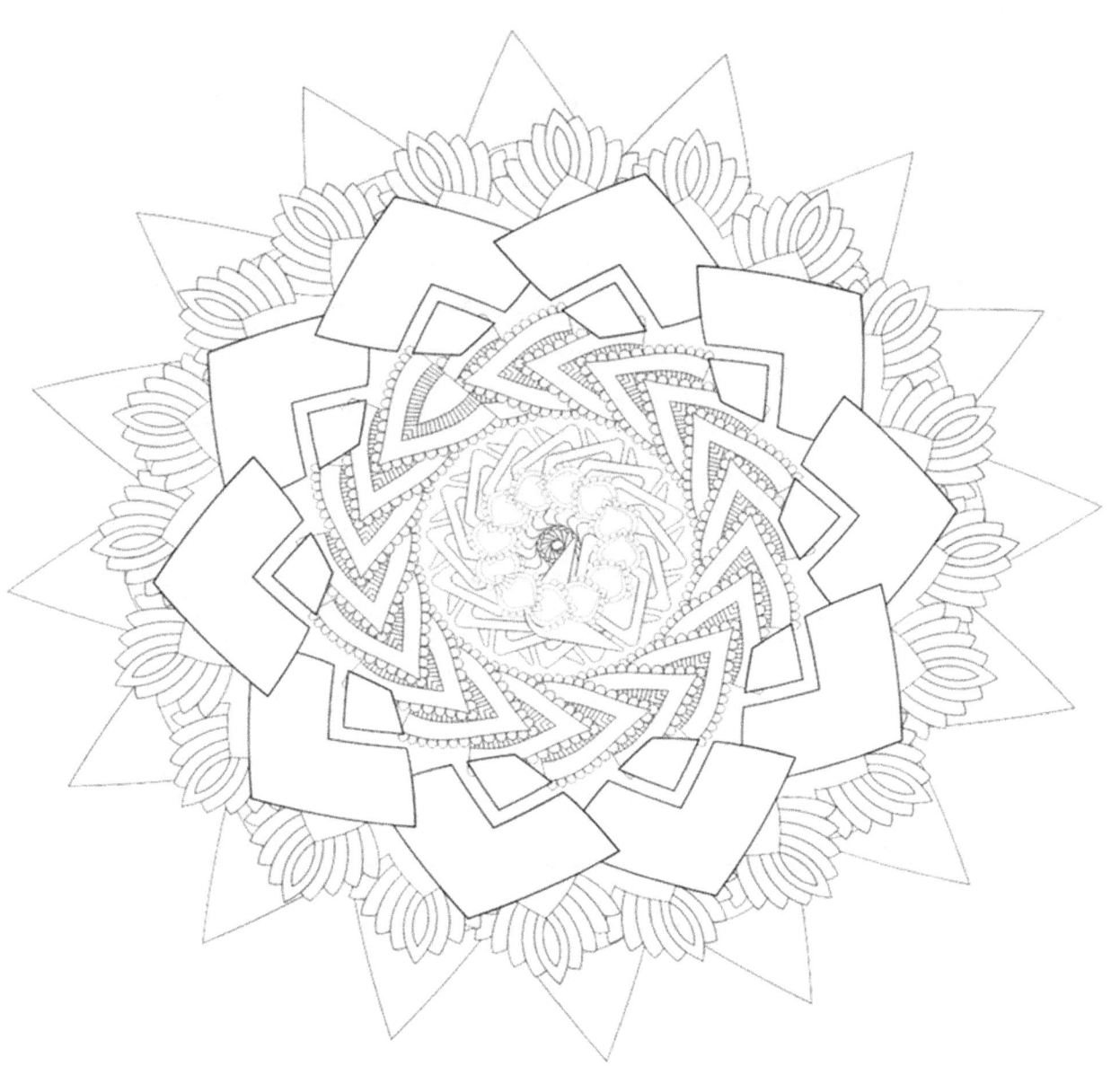

"Color helps to express light, not the physical phenomenon, but the only light that really exists, that in the artist's brain."
– Henri Matisse

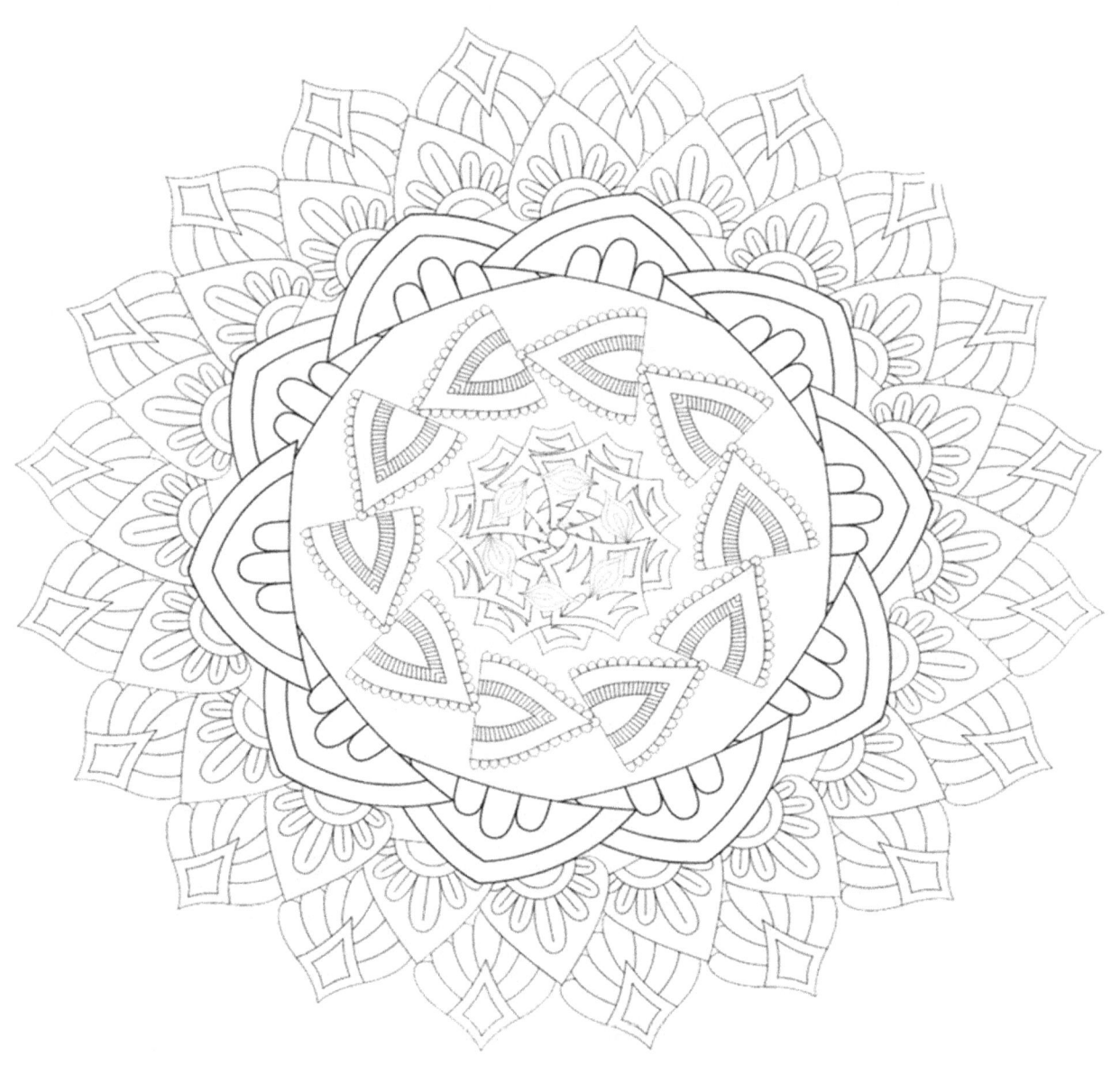

"Color is the place where our brain and the universe meet."
– Paul Klee

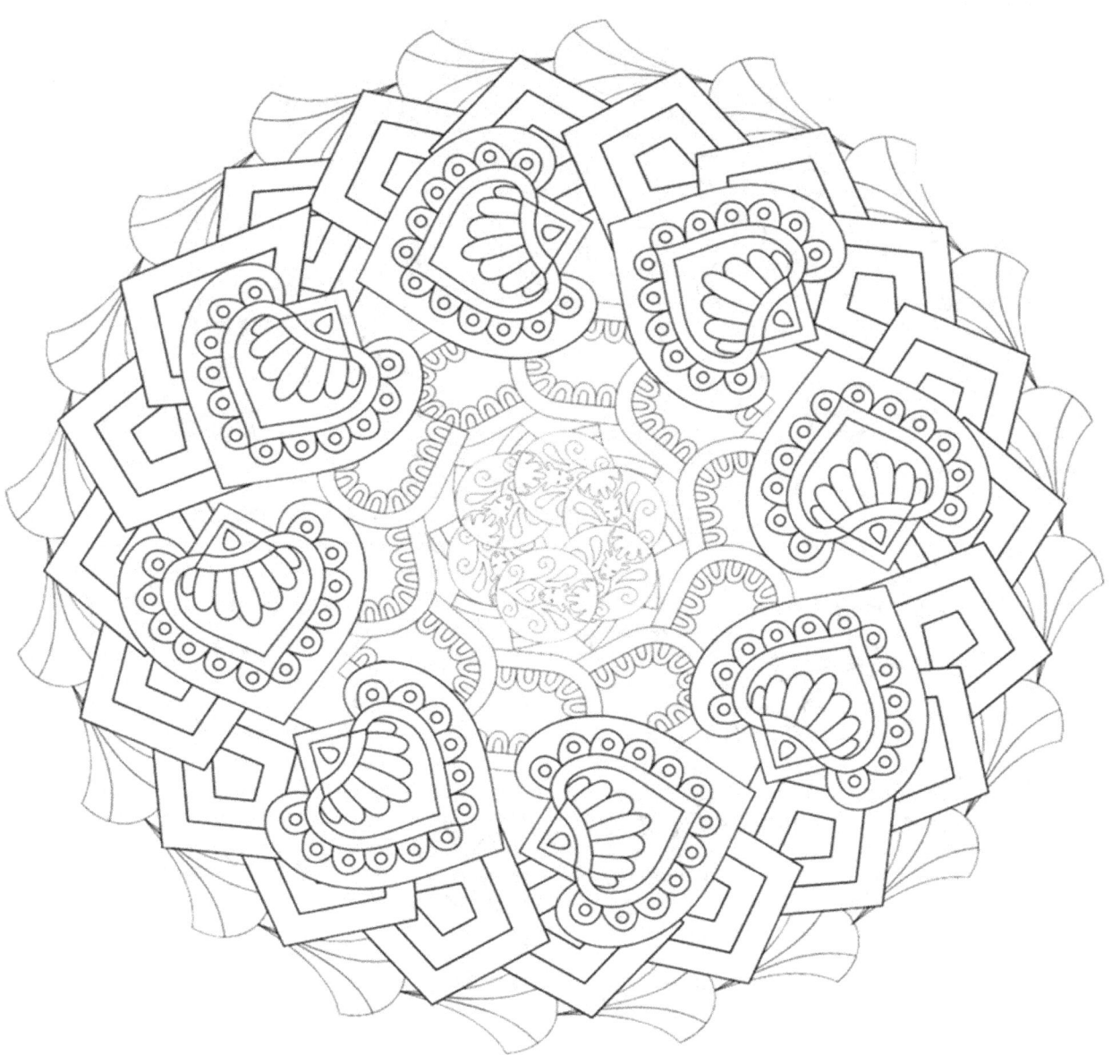

"Everything that you can see in the world around you presents itself to your eyes only as an arrangement of patches of different colors." – John Ruskin

"The fact that the colors in the flower have evolved in order to attract insects to pollinate it is interesting; that means insects can see the colors. That adds a question: does this aesthetic sense we have also exist in lower forms of life?"
– Richard P. Feynman

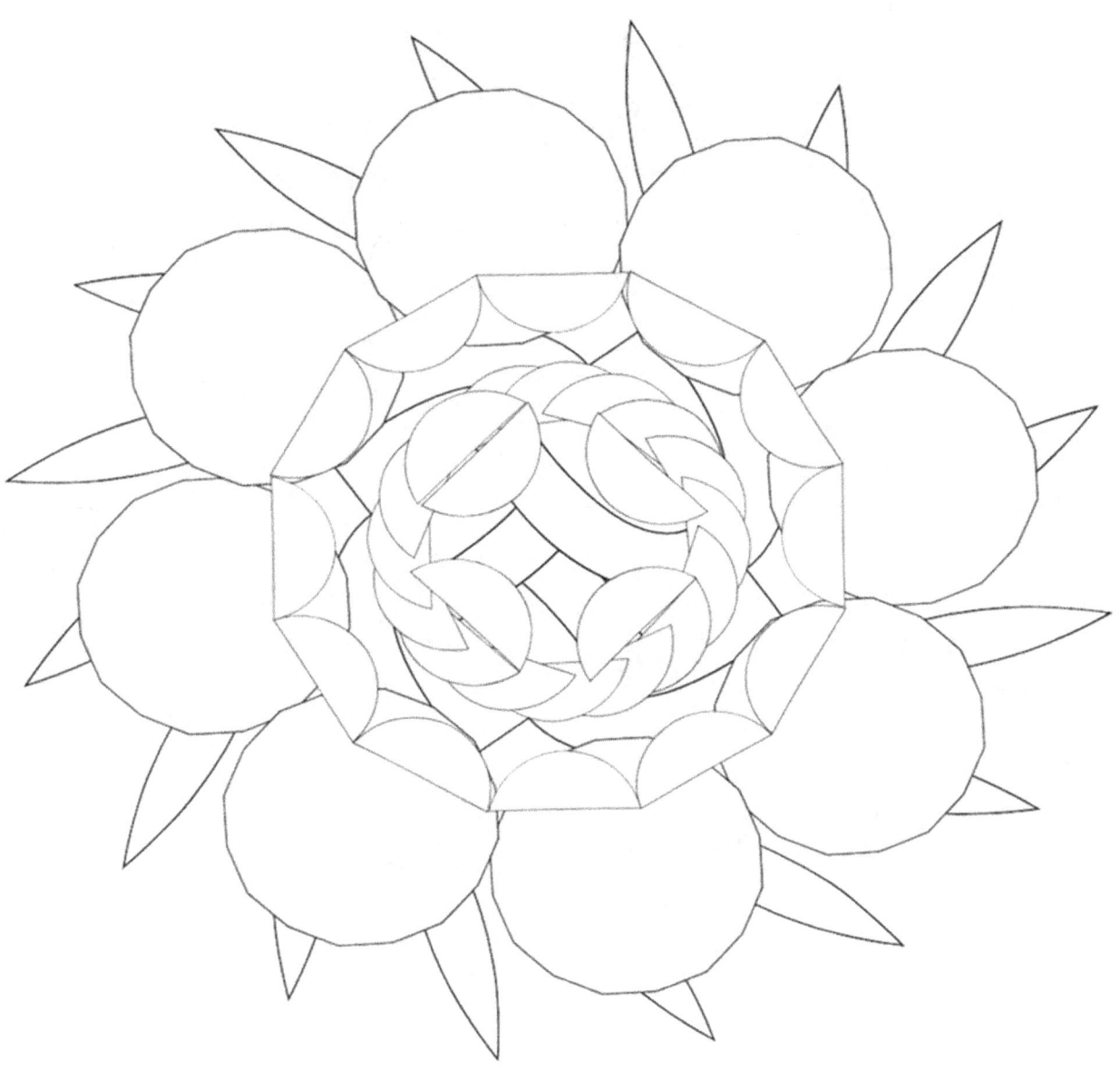

"The painter has to unlearn the habit of thinking that things seem to have the color which common sense says they 'really' have, and to learn the habit of seeing things as they appear."
– Bertrand Russell

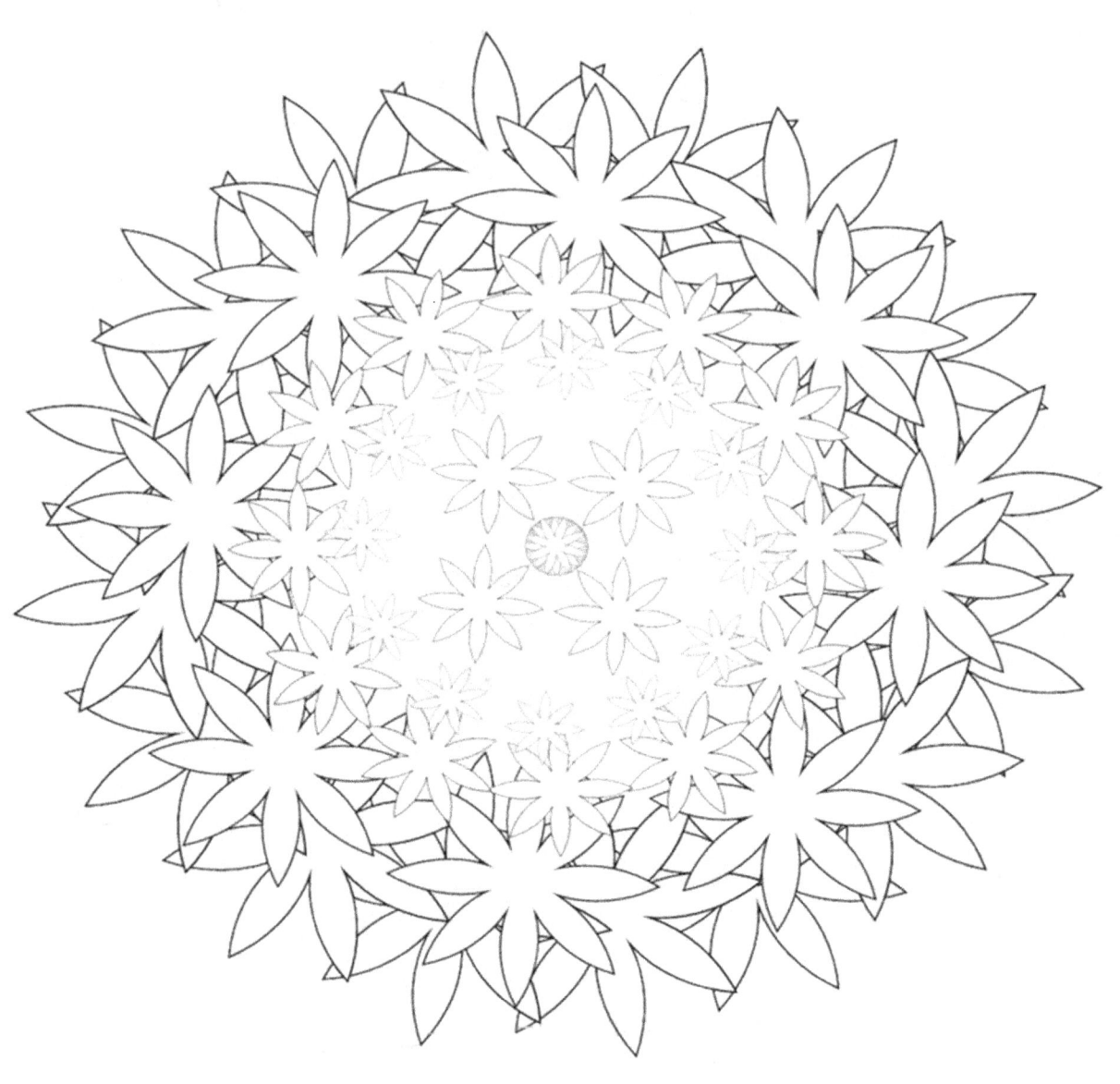

"Color creates, enhances, changes, reveals and establishes the mood of the painting."
— Kiff Holland

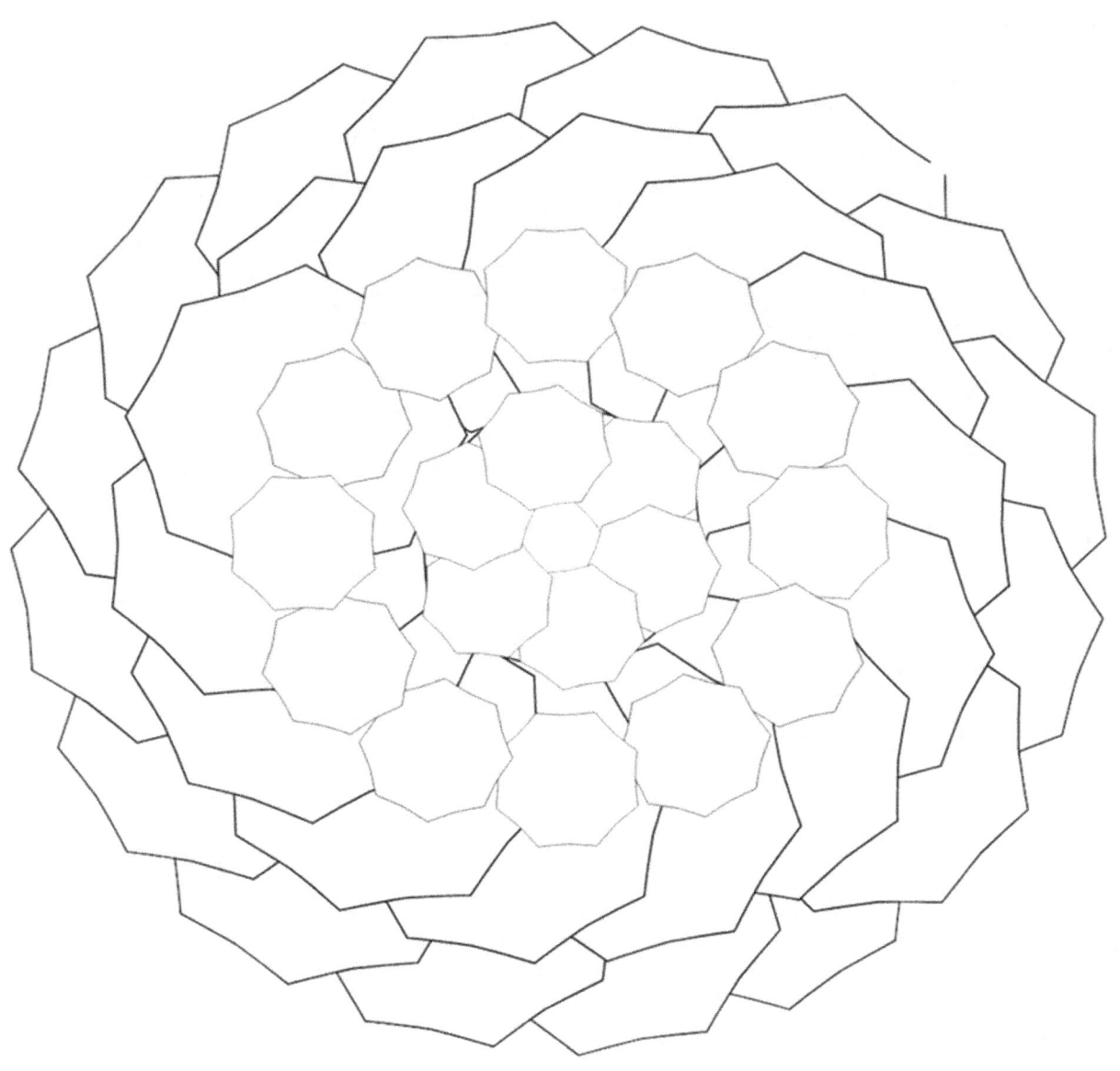

"Color is a power which directly influences the soul."
— Wassily Kandinsky

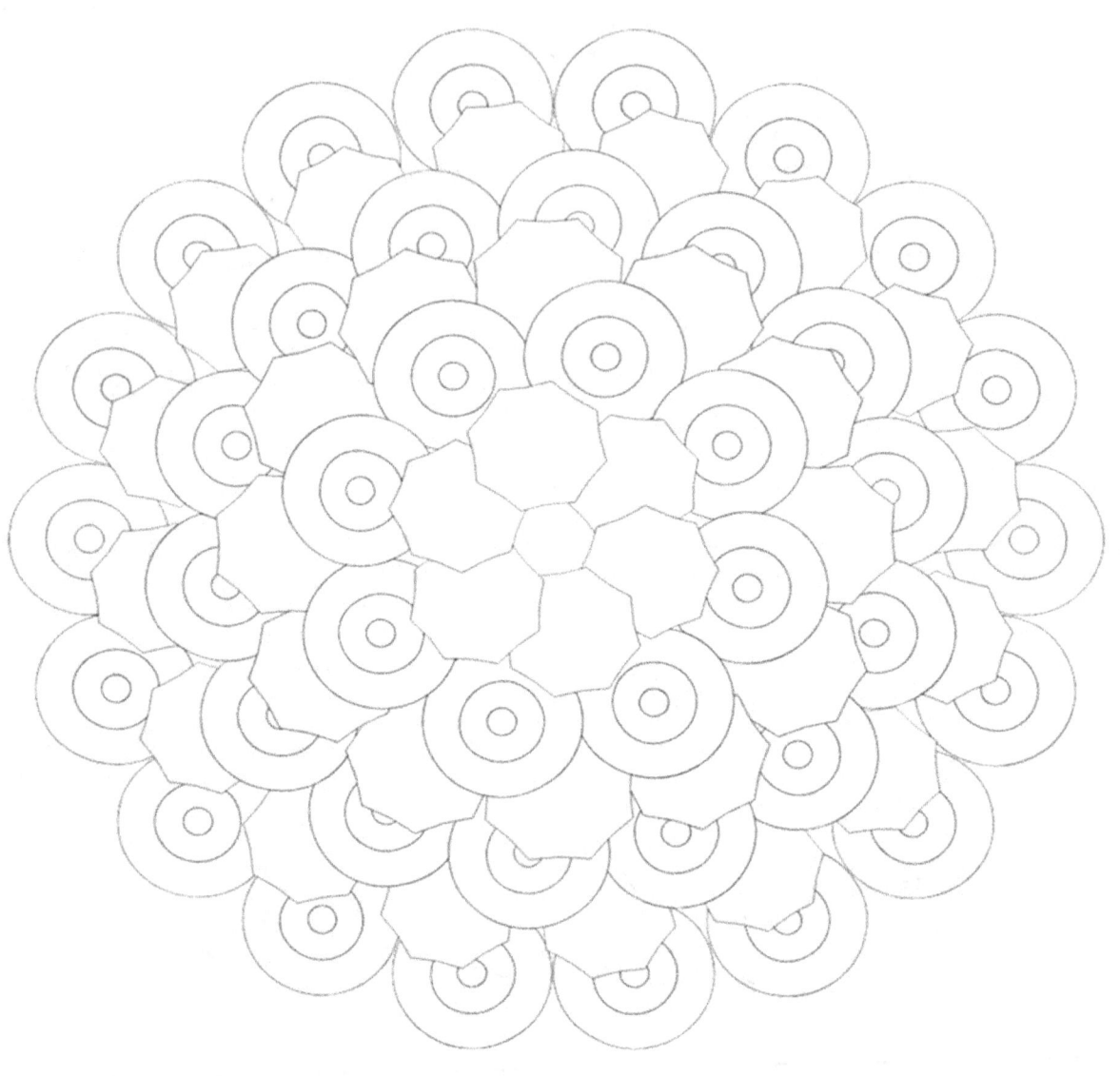

"The chief function of color should be to serve expression."
– Henri Matisse

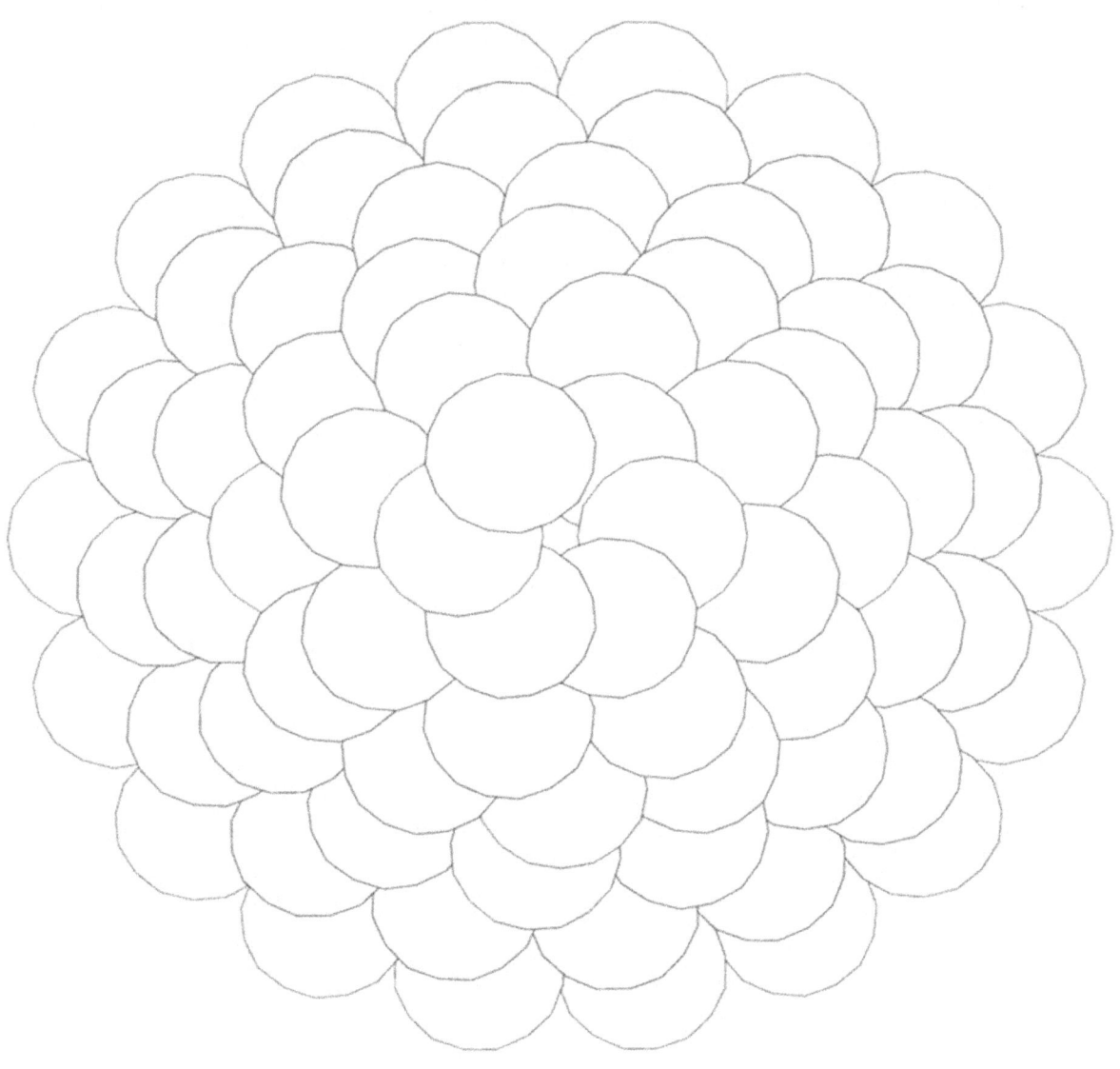

"Mere color, unspoiled by meaning, and unallied with definite form, can speak to the soul in a thousand different ways."
– Oscar Wilde

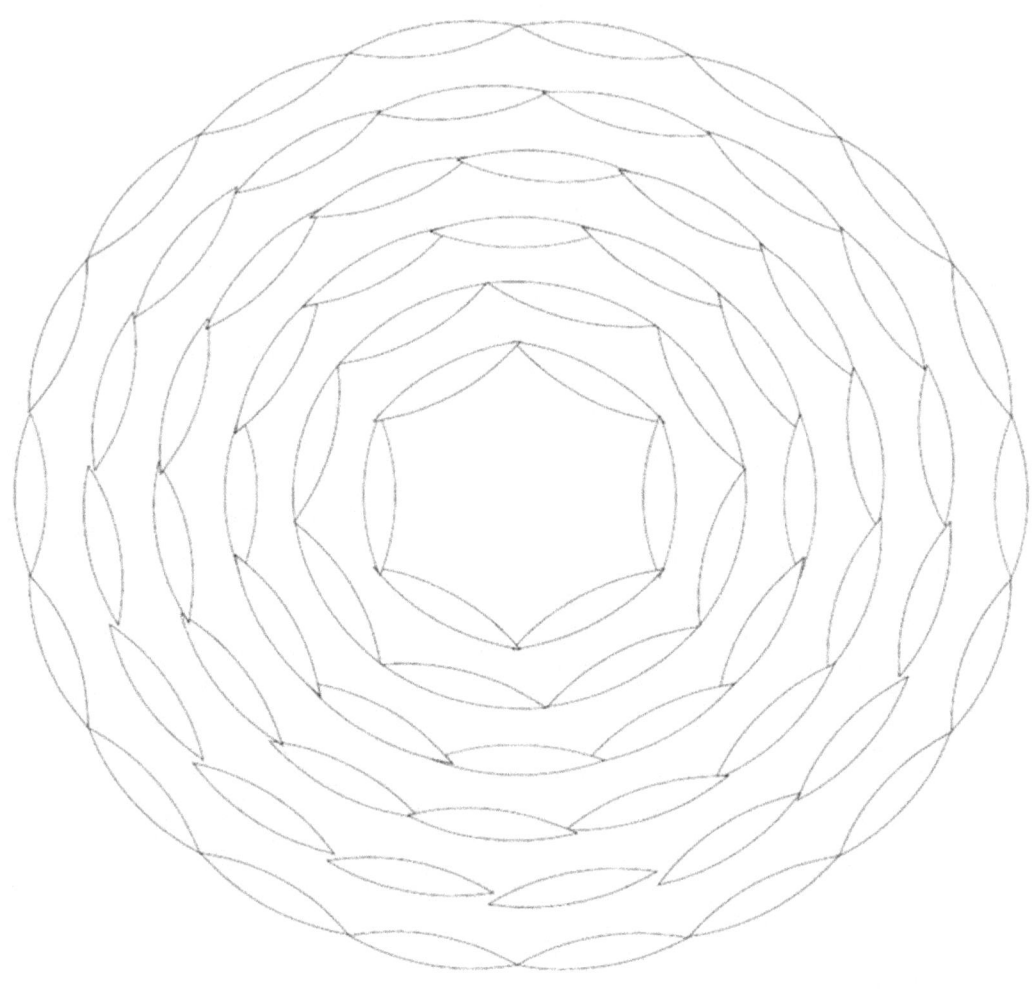

"Colors, like features, follow
the changes of the emotions."
– Pablo Picasso

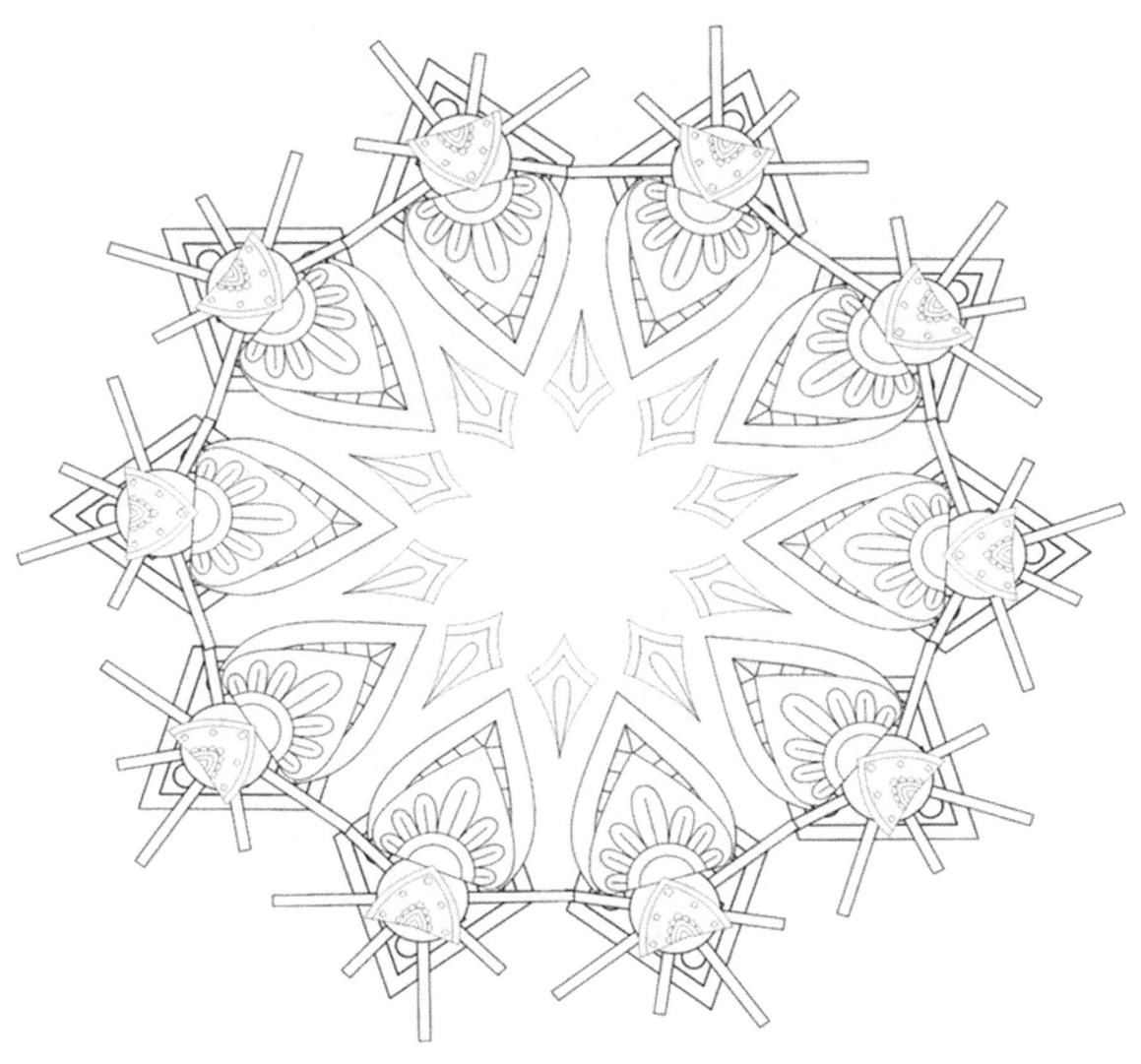

"All colors arouse specific
associative ideas..."
– Yves Klein

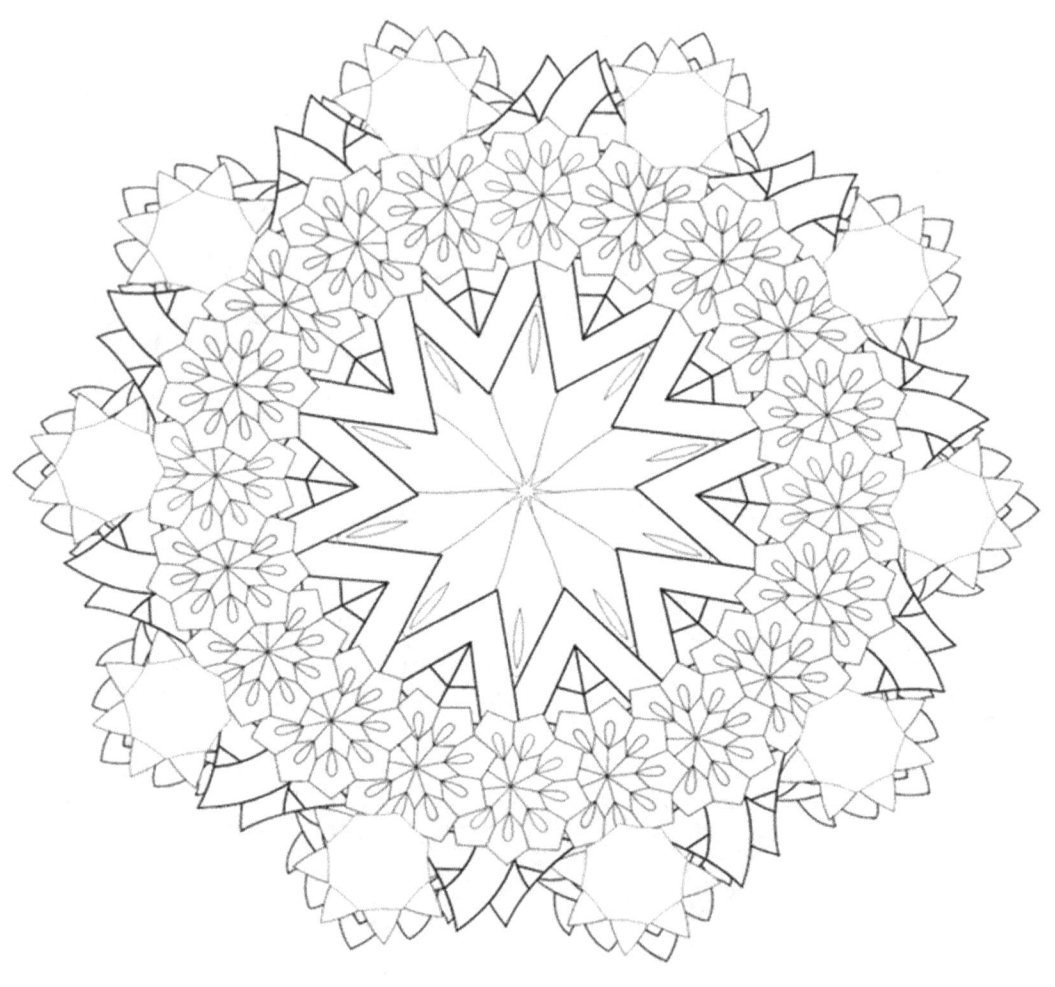

"Color provokes a psychic vibration. Color hides a power still unknown but real, which acts on every part of the human body."
– Wassily Kandinsky

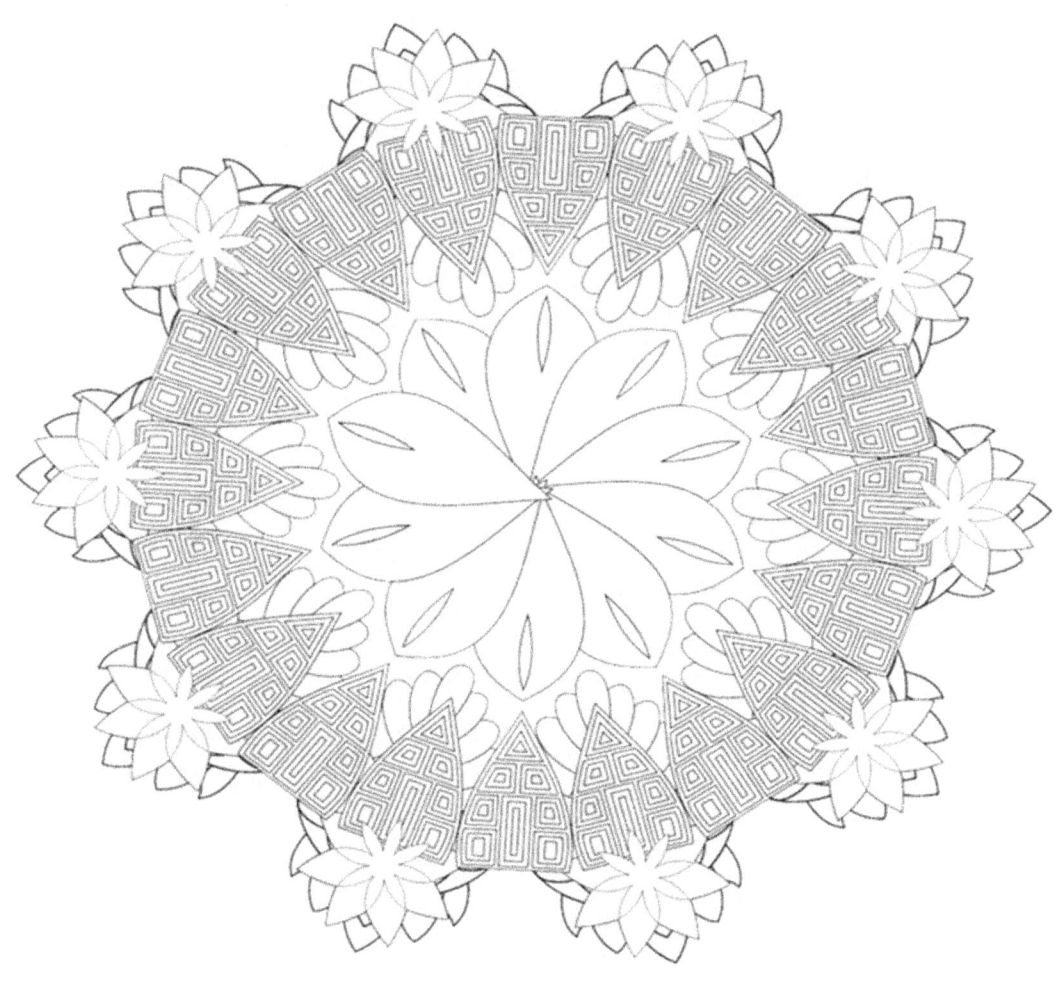

"Colors produce a corresponding spiritual vibration, and it is only as a step towards this spiritual vibration that the elementary physical impression is of importance."
– Wassily Kandinsky

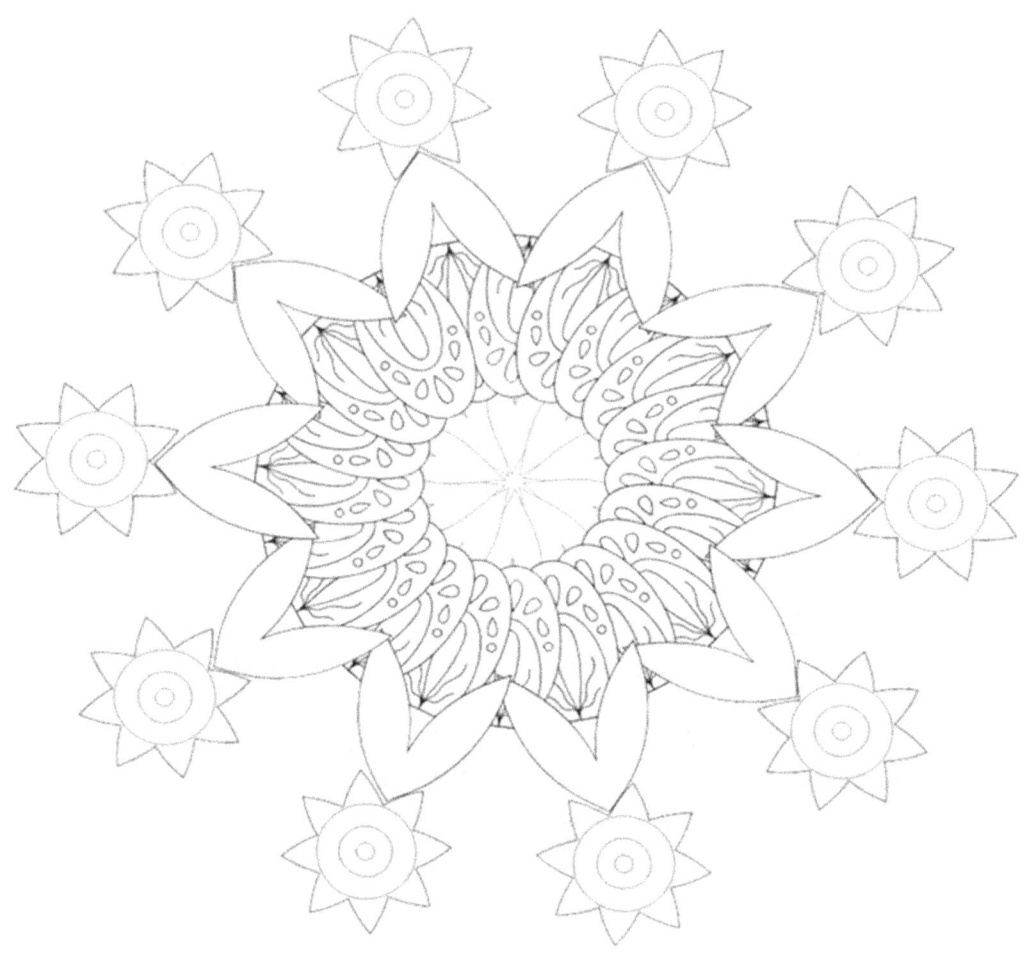

"Colors express the main psychic functions of man."
— Carl Gustav Jung

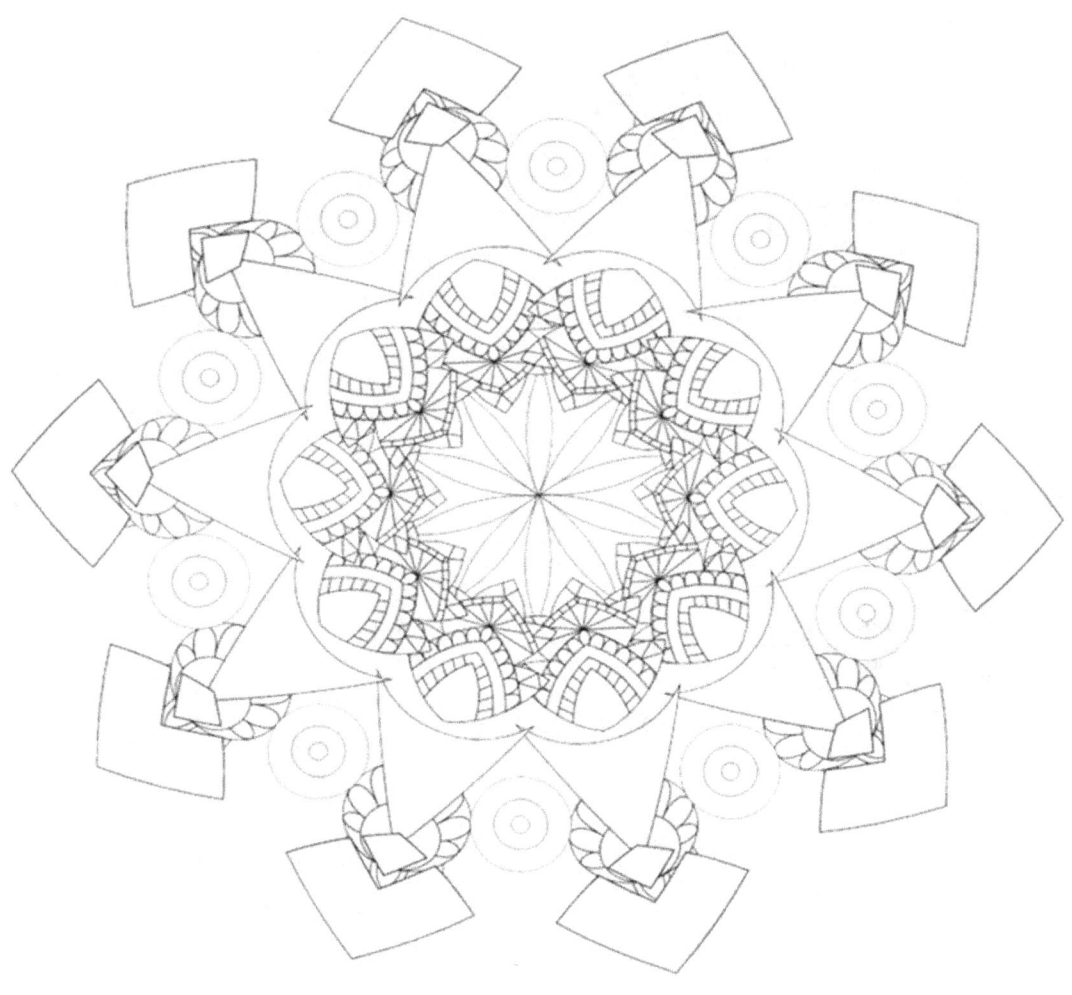

"Color! What a deep and mysteriou
language, the language of dreams."
— Paul Gauguin

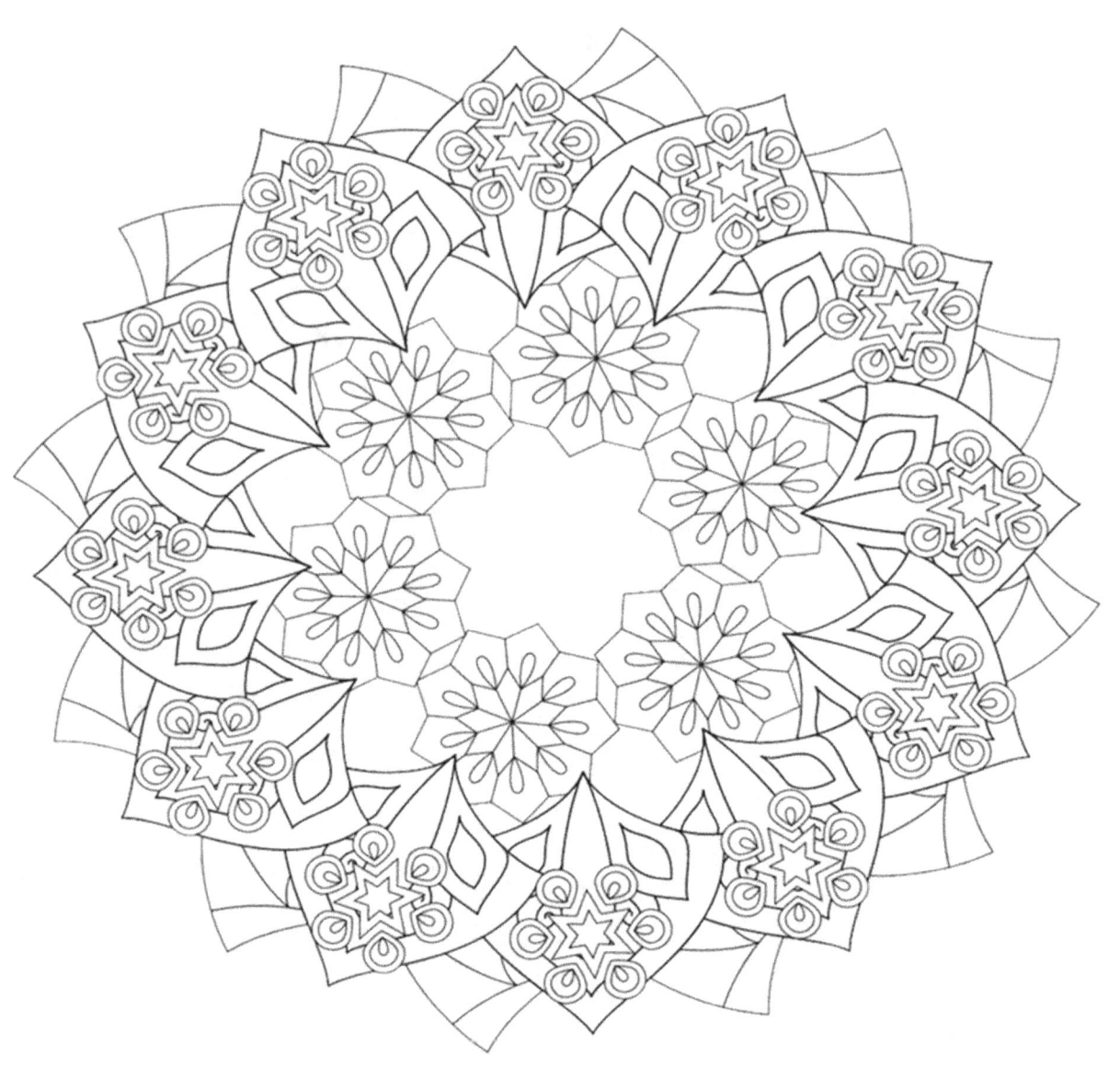

"Colors speak all languages."
– Joseph Addison

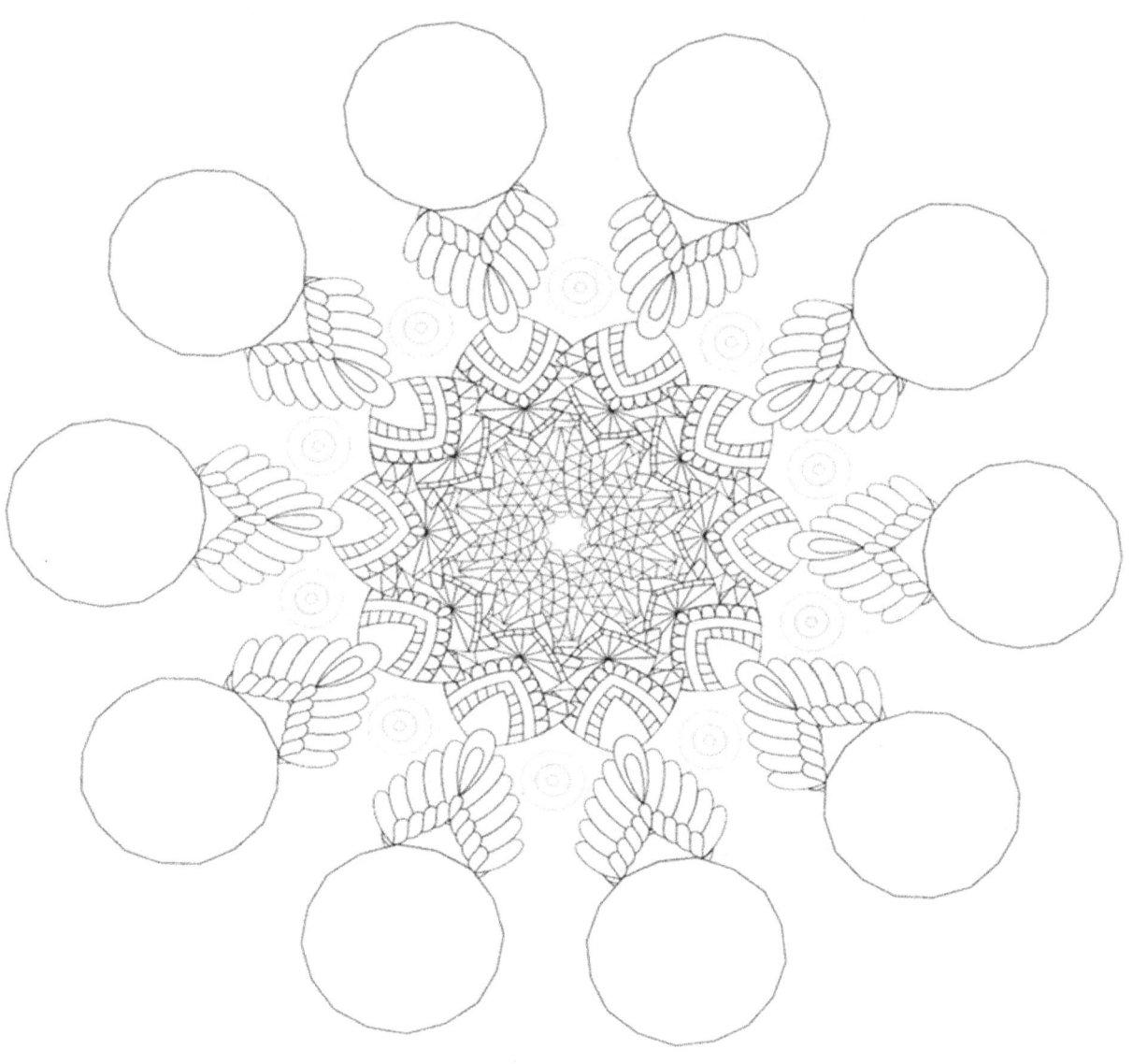

"If light is the spiritual quality of painting, color is surely its heart and passion."
– Robert Reynolds

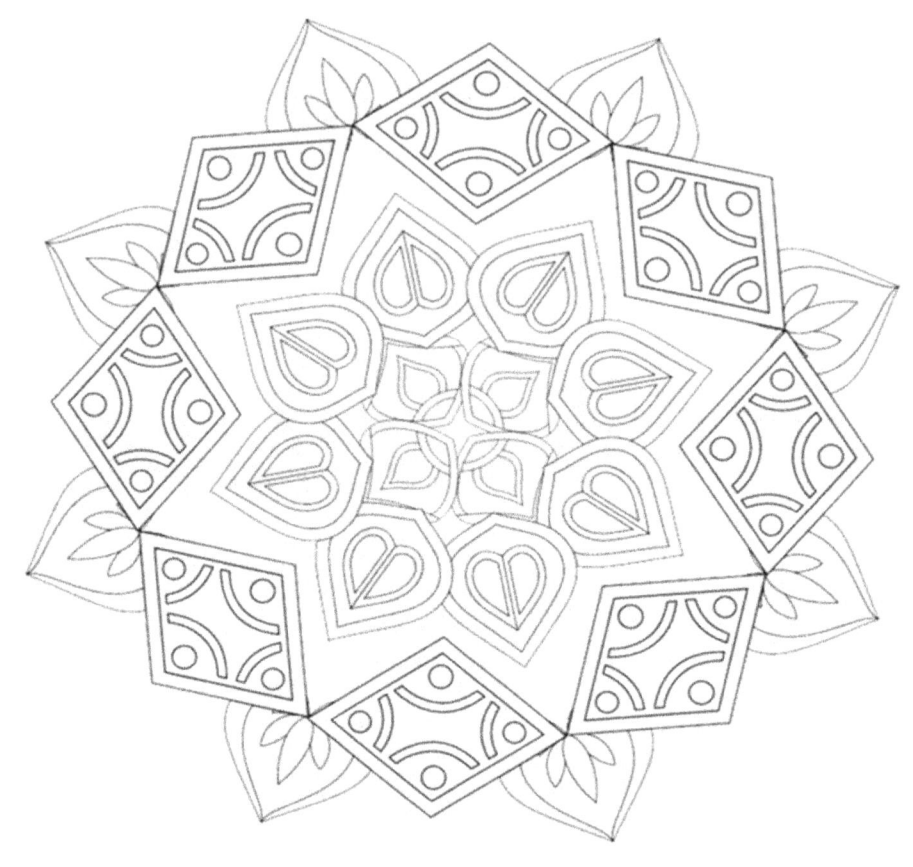

"Be sensitive to your sensitive inner capacities to respond to color."
– Nathan Cabot Hale

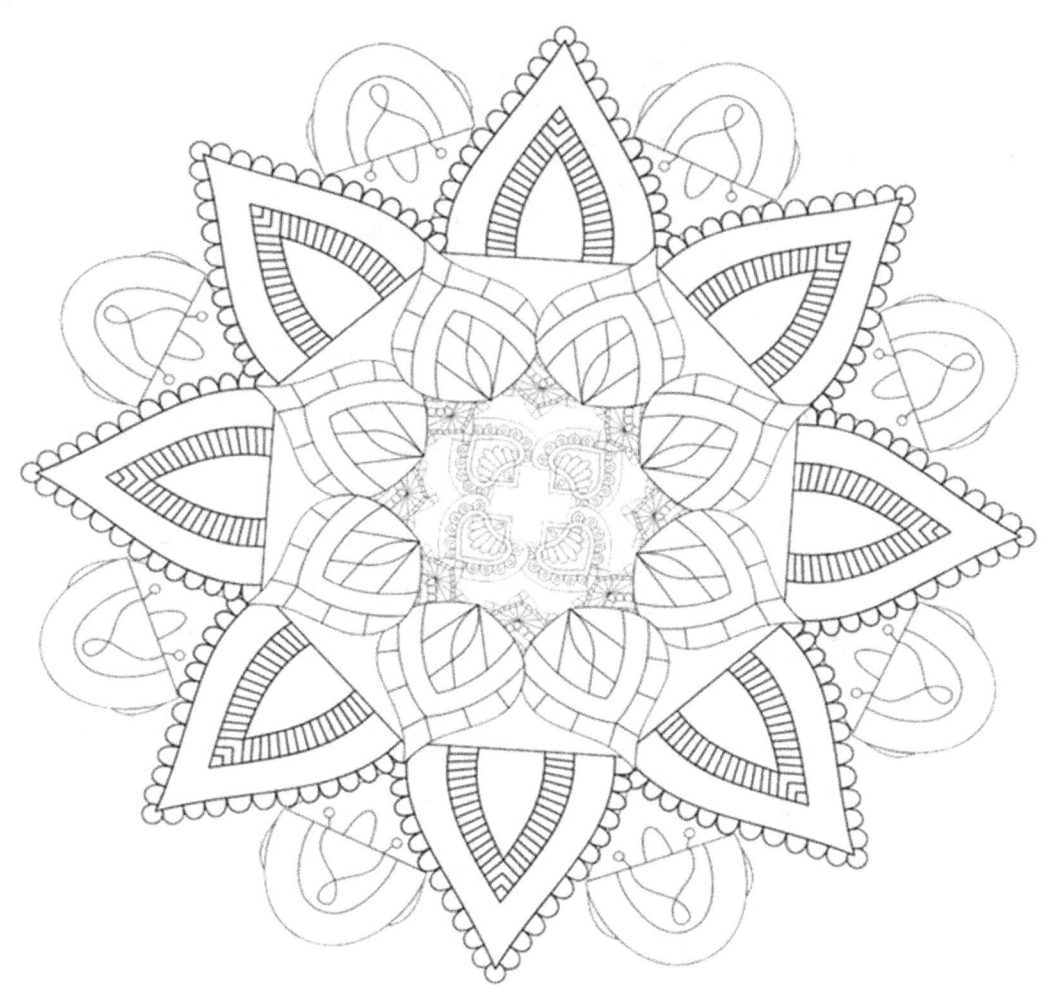

"The artist's alertness to the coloristic demands of each picture, the ability to respond to the picture's needs, to feed the color until its appetite is satiated; these are the true measures of a colorist's talent."
– Wolf Kahn

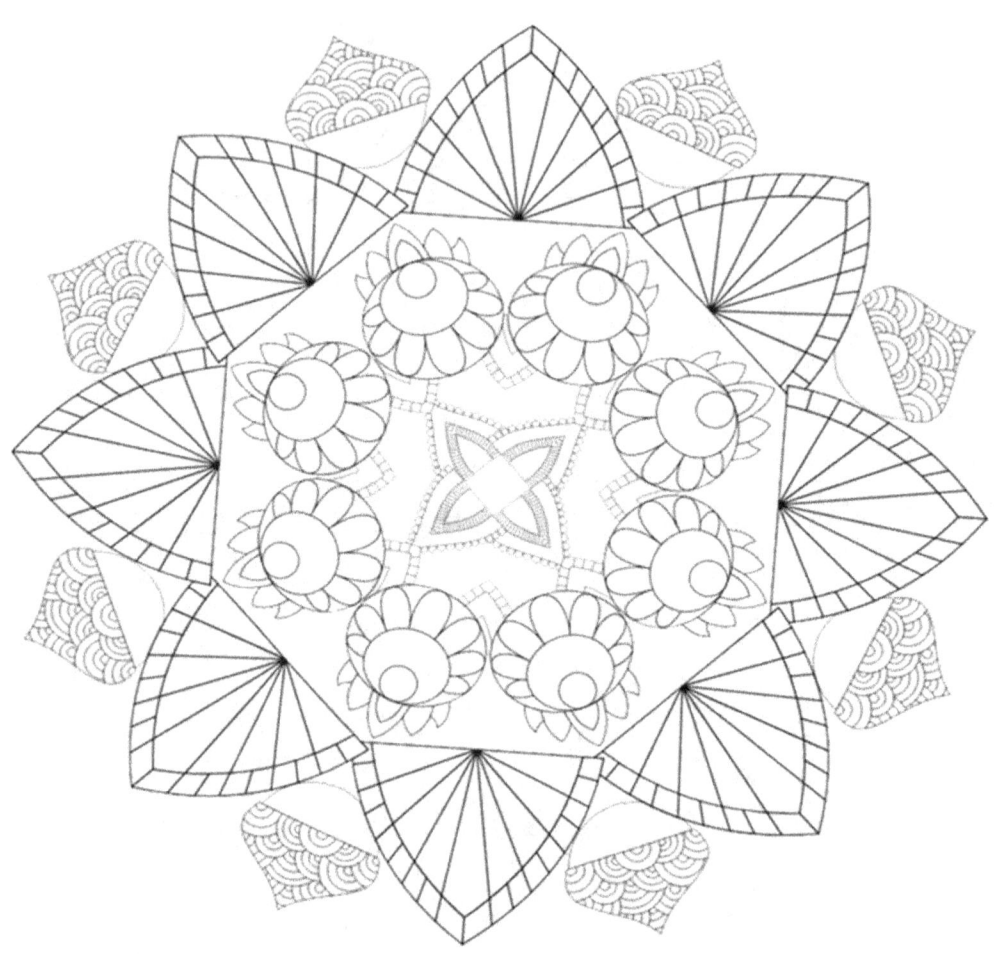

"Color is my day-long obsession, joy and torment. To such an extent indeed that one day, finding myself at the deathbed of a woman who had been and still was very dear to me, I caught myself in the act of focusing on her temples and automatically analyzing the succession of appropriately graded colors which death was imposing on her motionless face."
– Claude Monet

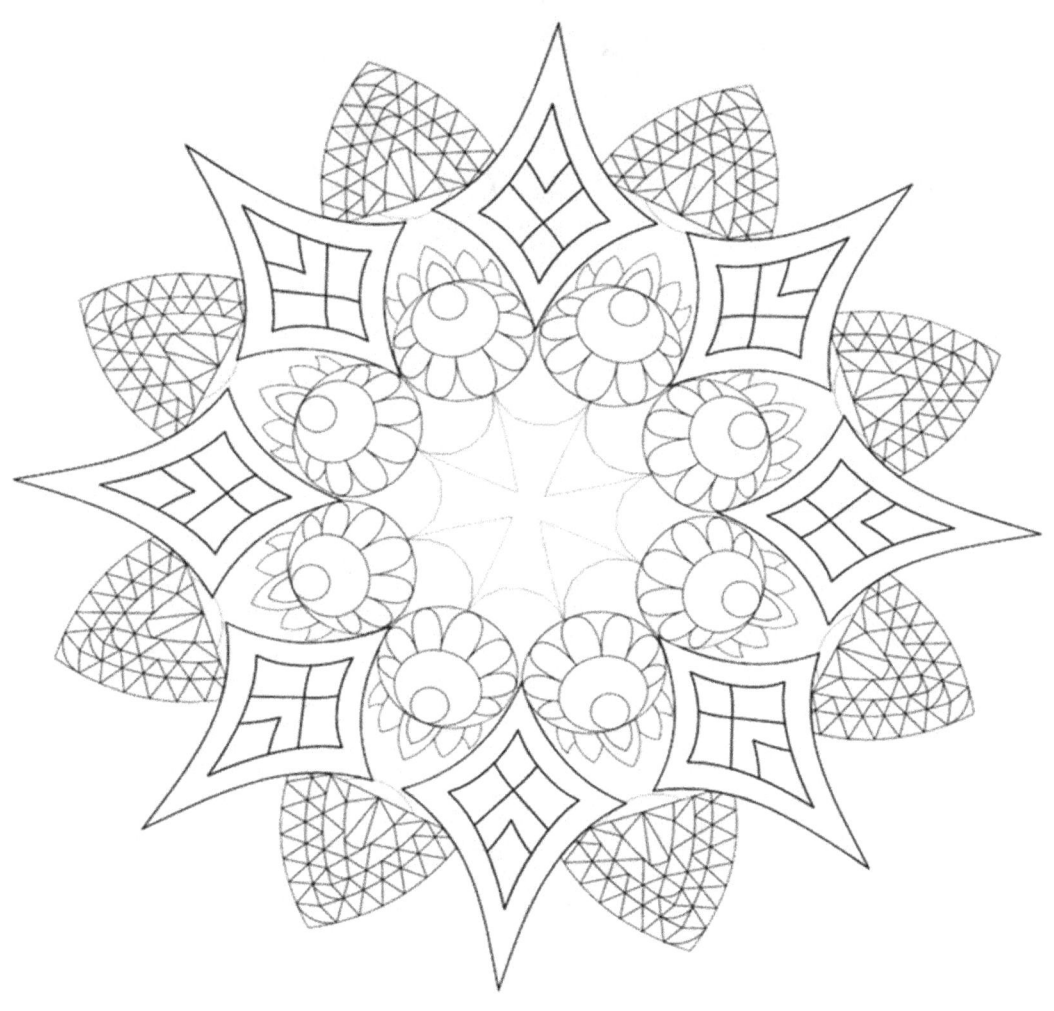

"Not only can color, which is under fixed laws, be taught like music, but it is easier to learn than drawing, whose elaborate principles cannot be taught."
— Eugene Delacroix

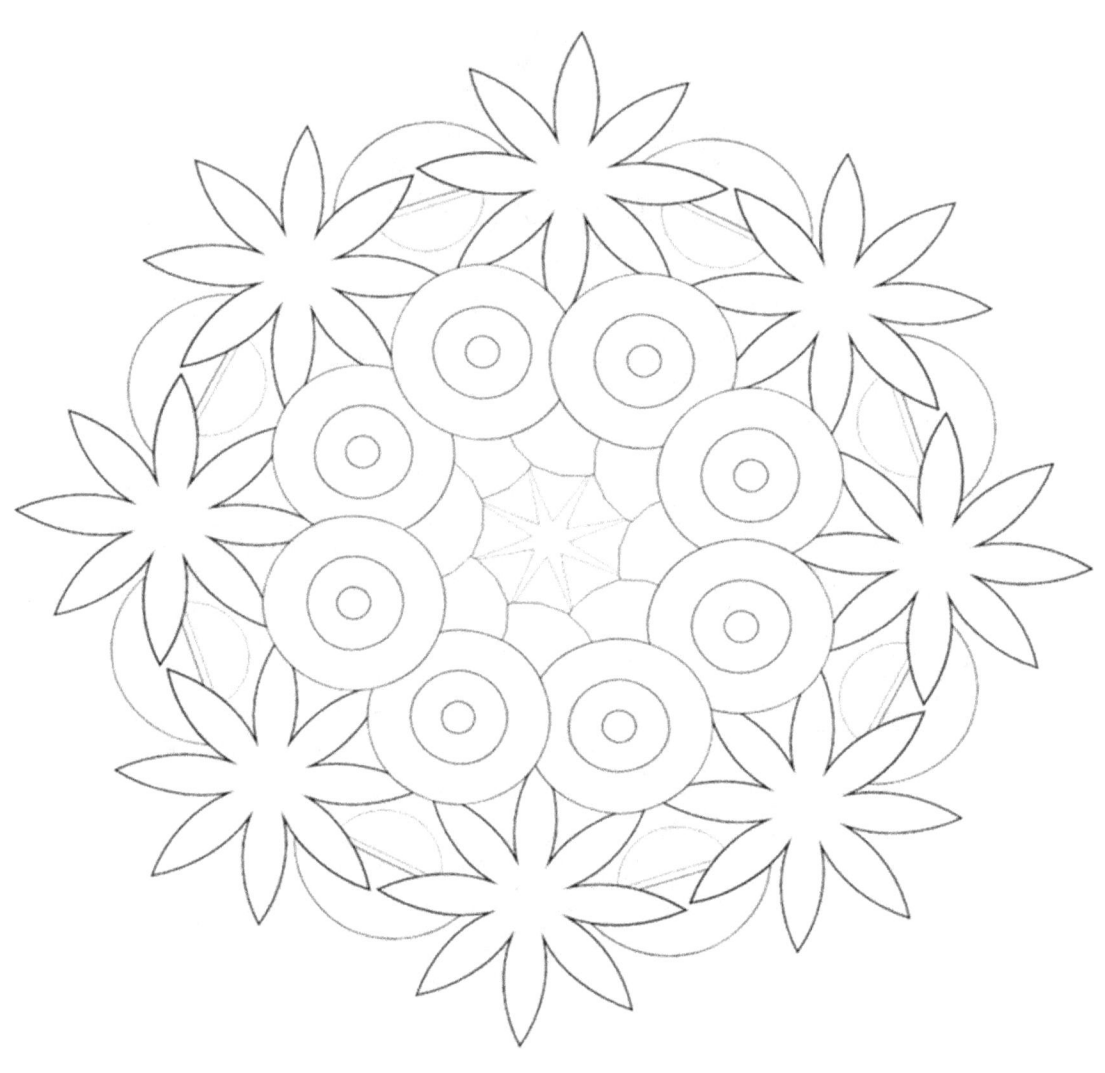

"There is a logic of colors, and it is with this alone, and not with the logic of the brain, that the painter should conform."
– Paul Cezanne

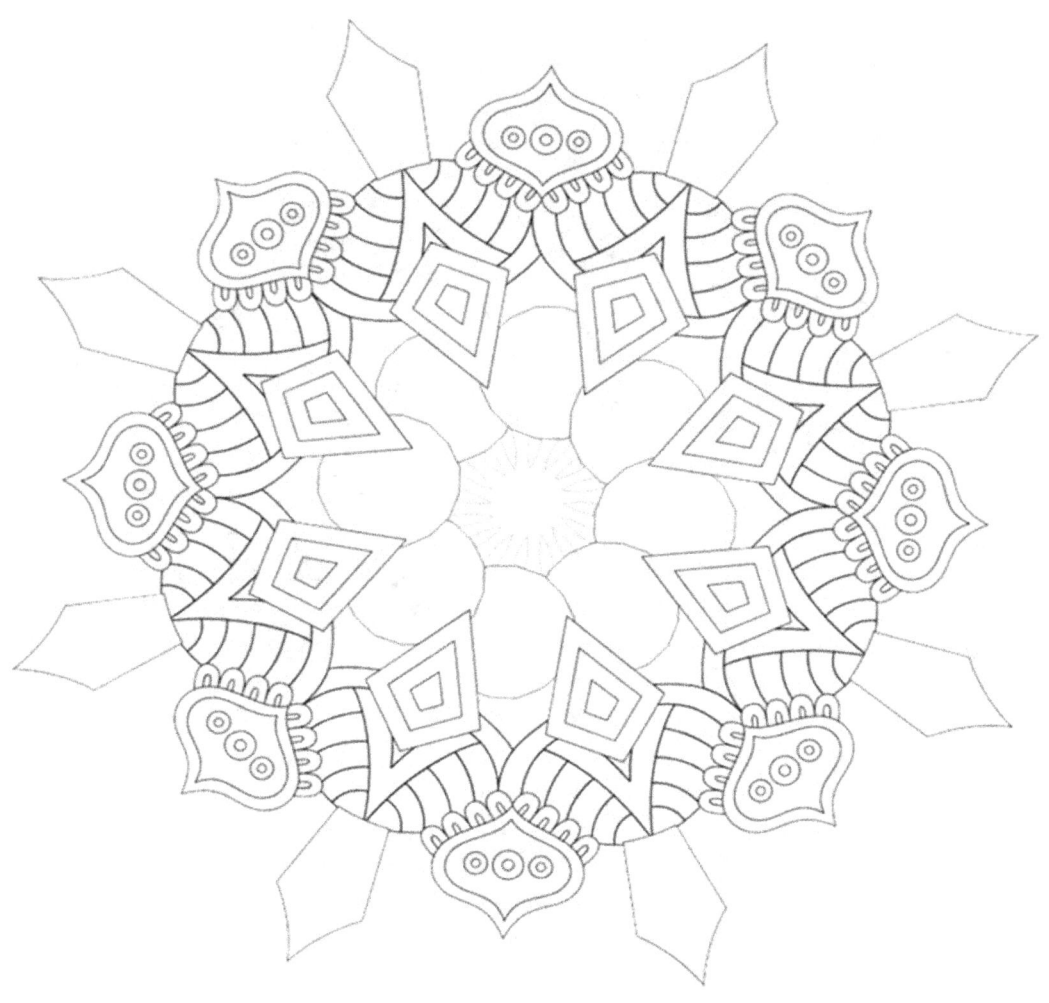

"If one could only catch that true color of nature – the very thought of it drives me mad."
– Andrew Wyeth

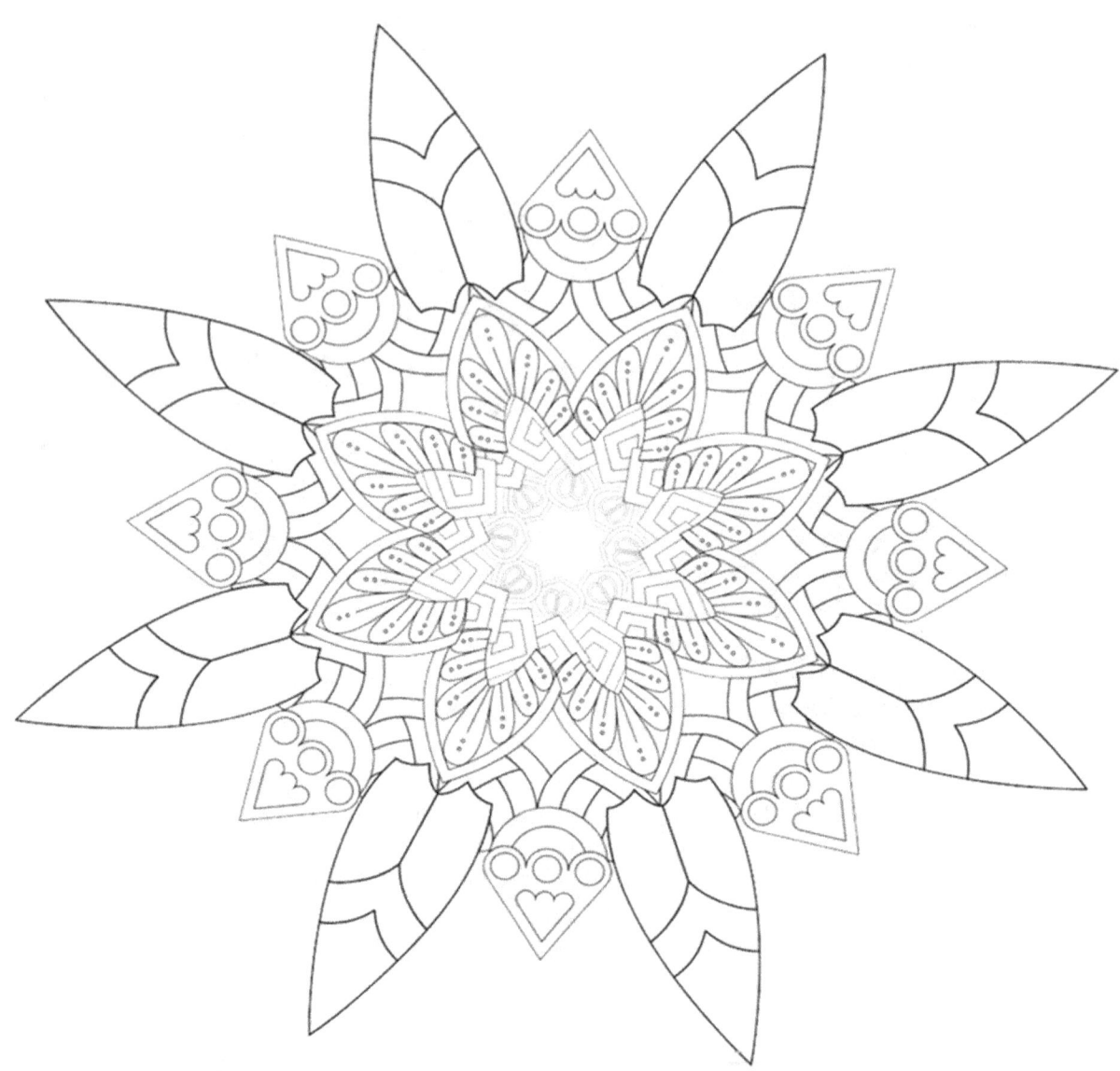

"In an atmosphere of uniform density the most distant things seen through it, such as the mountains, in consequence of the great quantity of atmosphere which is between your eye and them, will appear blue. Therefore you should make the building... wall which is more distant less defined and bluer... five times as far away, make five times as blue."
– Leonardo da Vinci

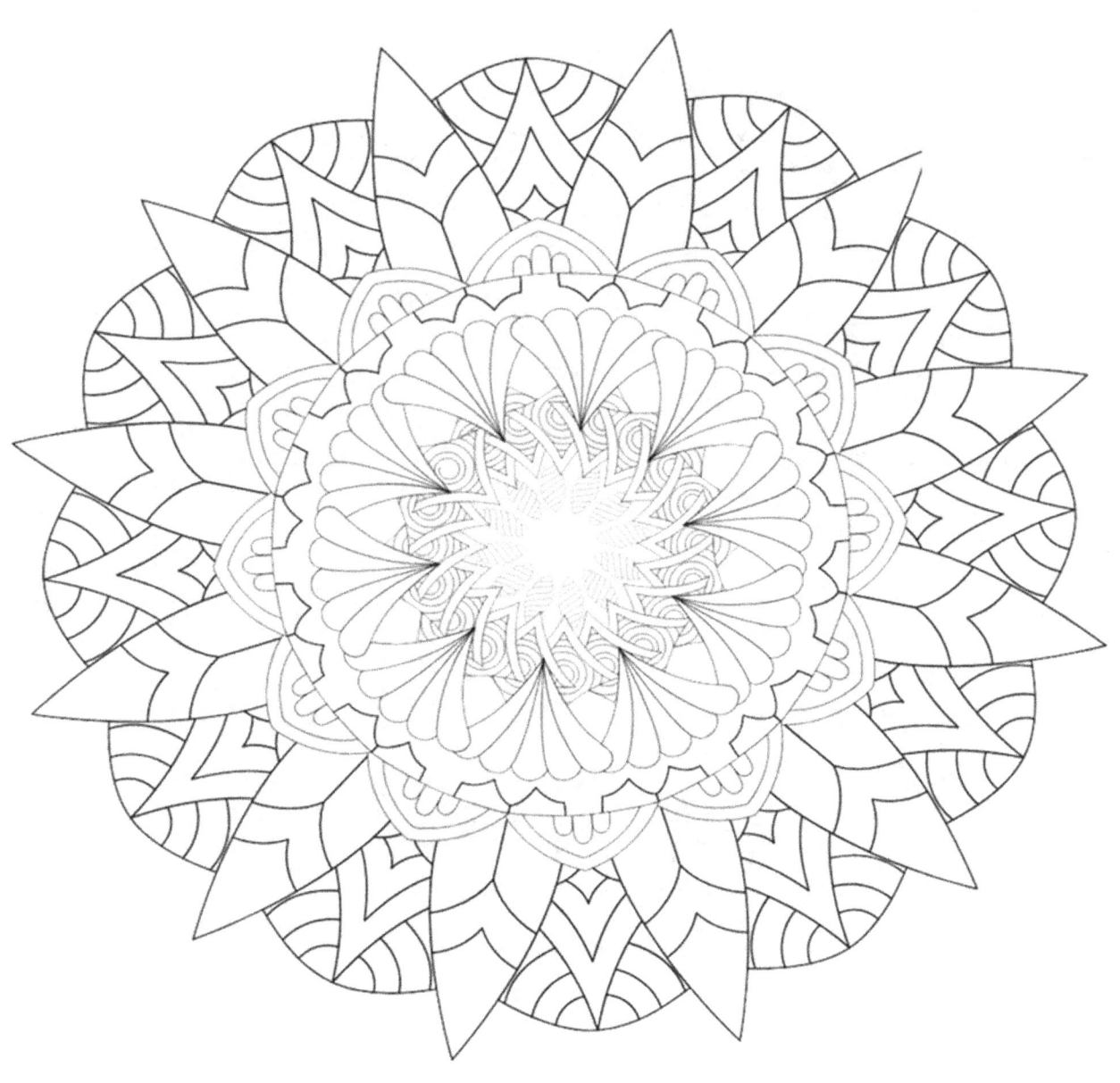

"Color is so much a matter of direct and immediate perception that any discussion of theory needs to be accompanied by experiments with the colors themselves."
– Walter Sargent

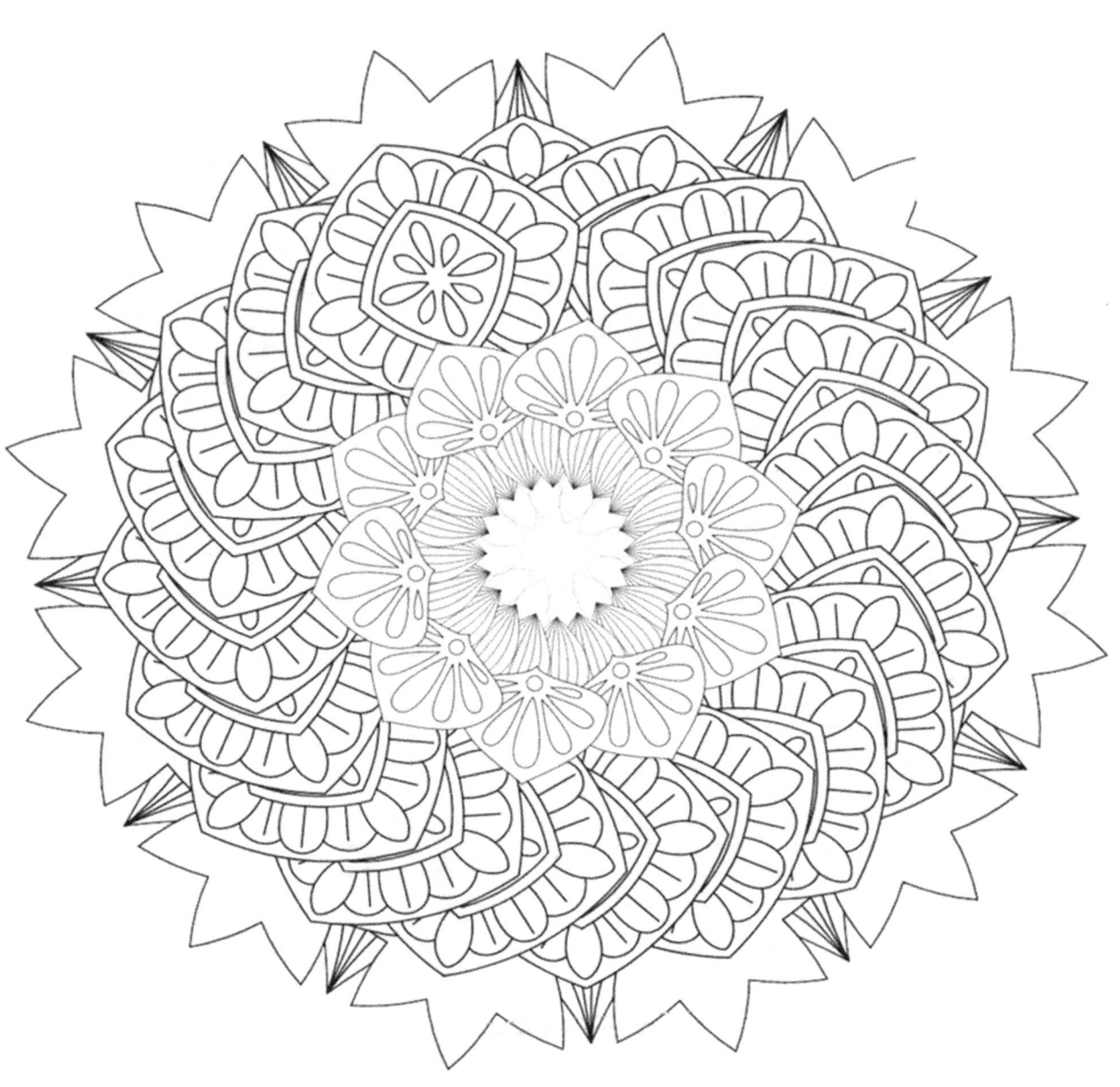

"He who wishes to become a master of color must see, feel, and experience each individual color in its endless combinations with all other colors."
– Johannes Itten

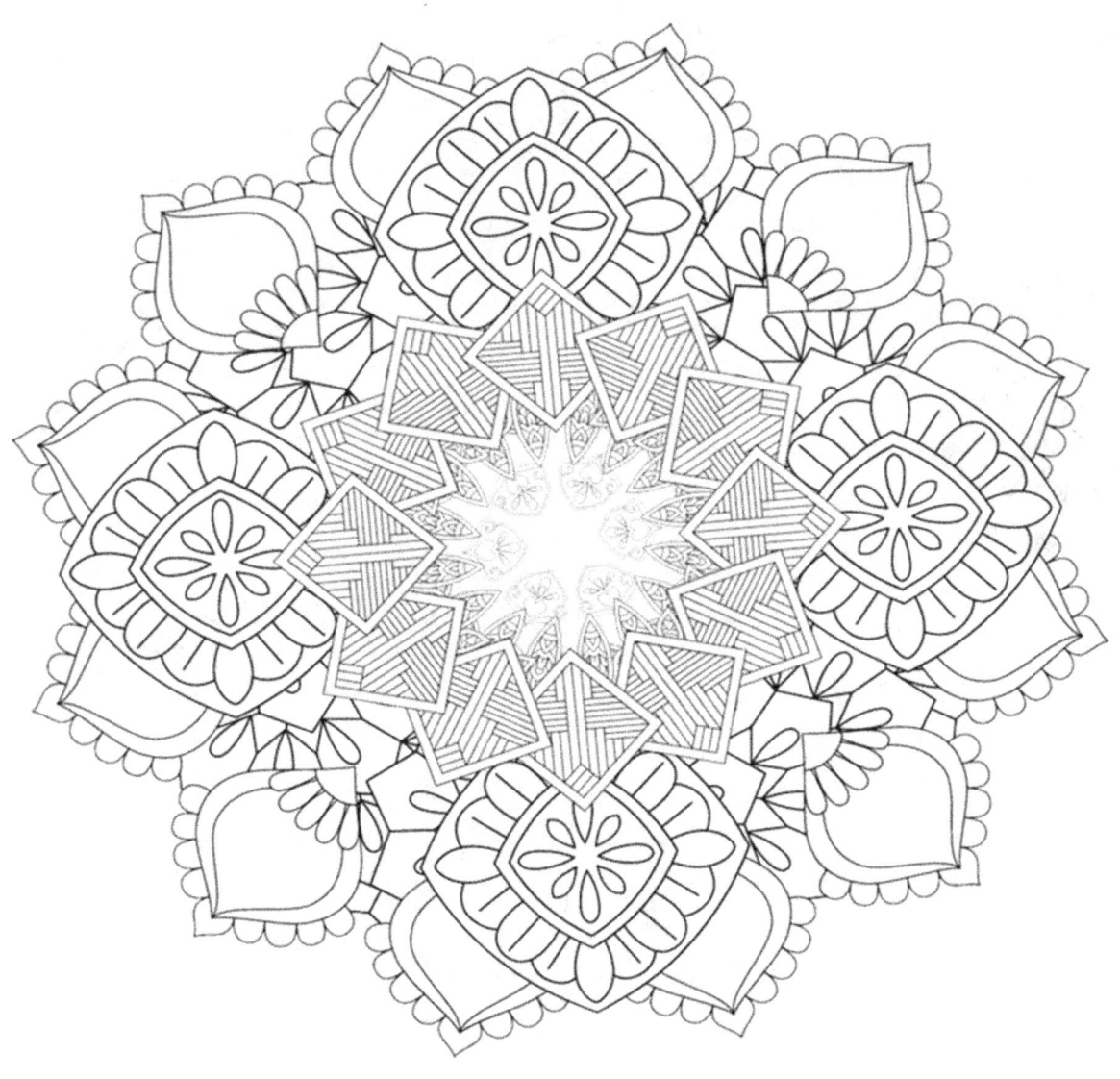

"In order to change a color it is enough to change the color of its background."
– Michel Eugene Chevreul

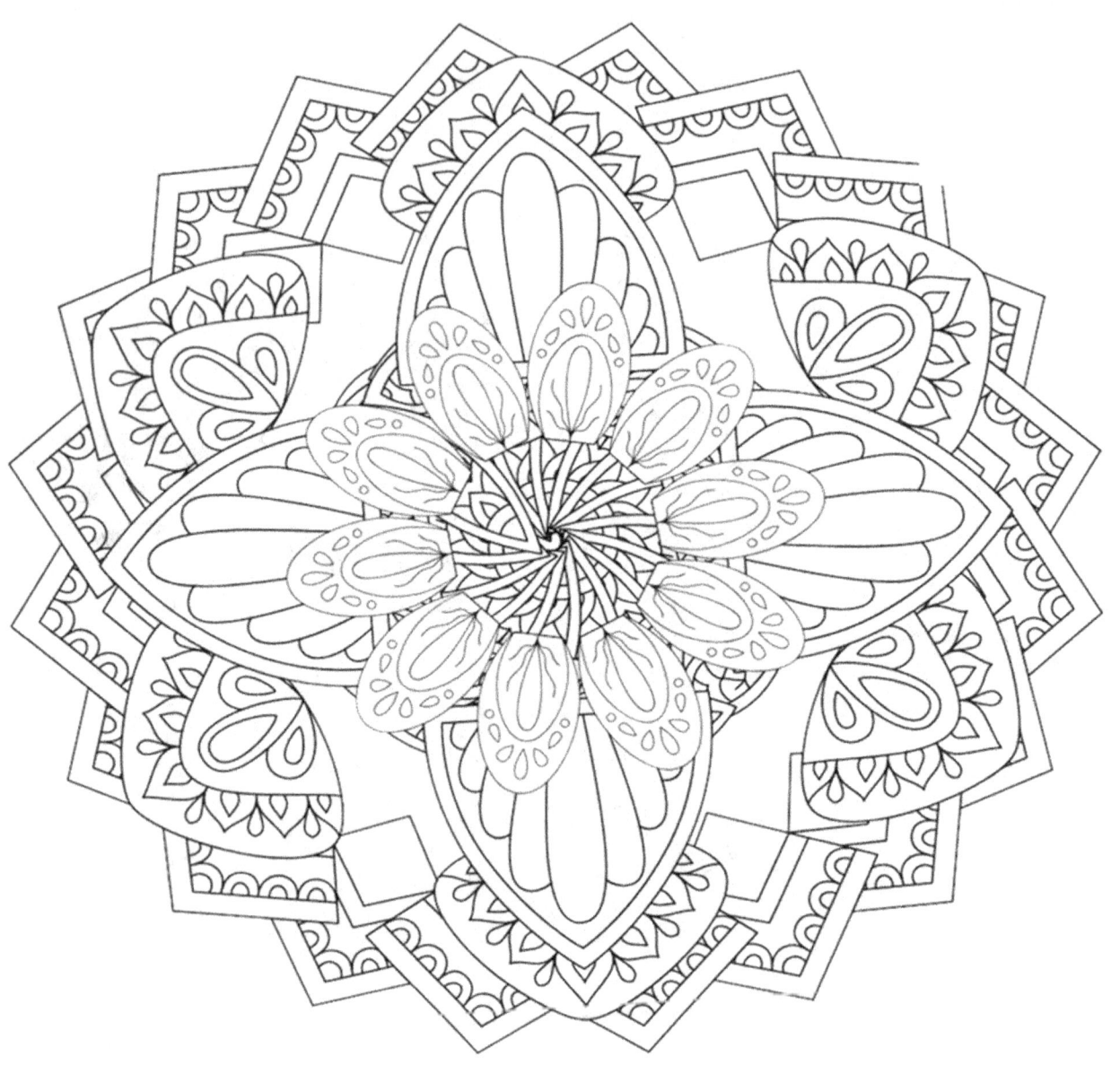

"All colors are the friends of their neighbors
and the lovers of their opposites."
- Marc Chagall

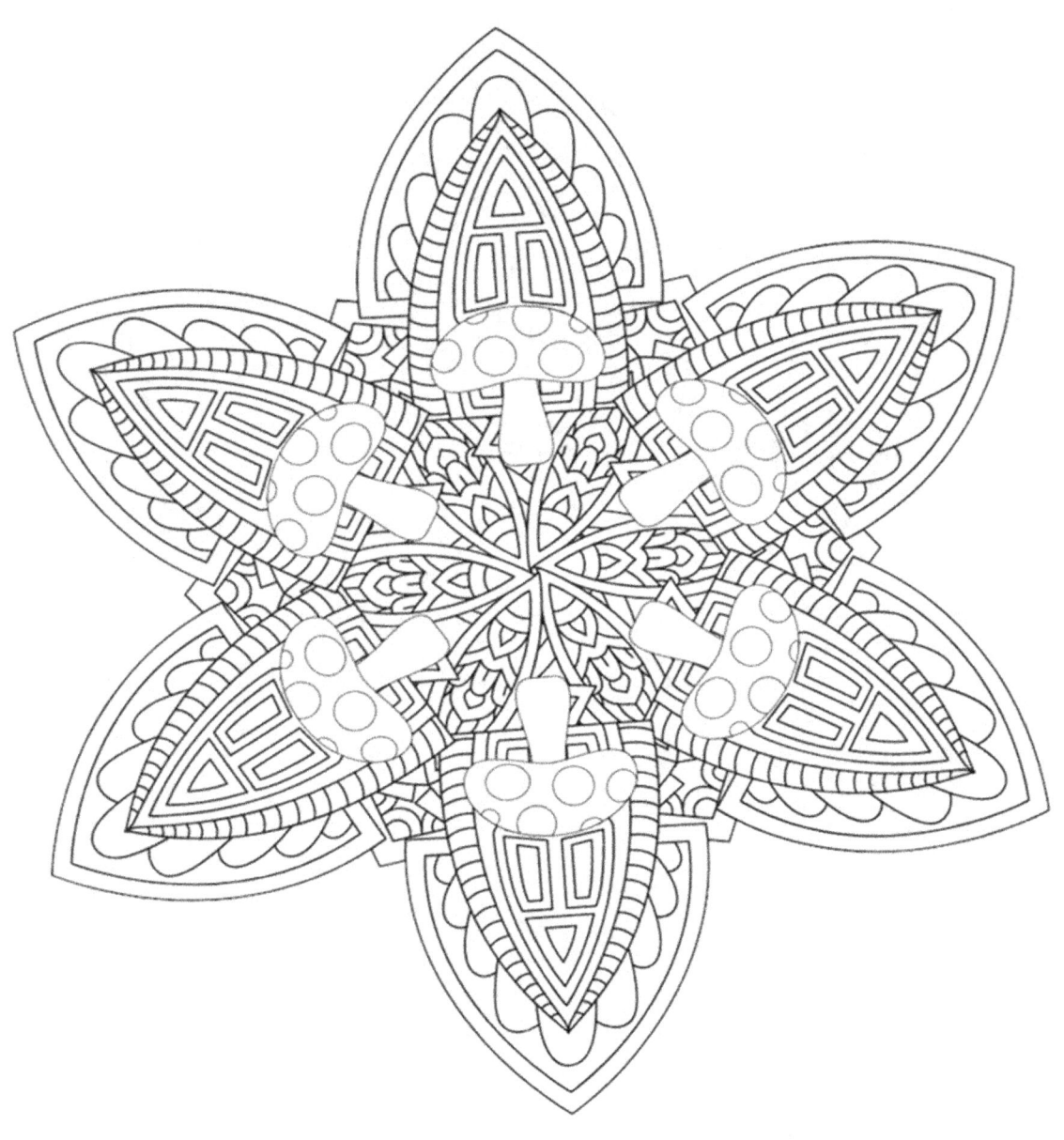

"Why do two colors, put one next to the other, sing? Can one really explain this?"
– Pablo Picasso

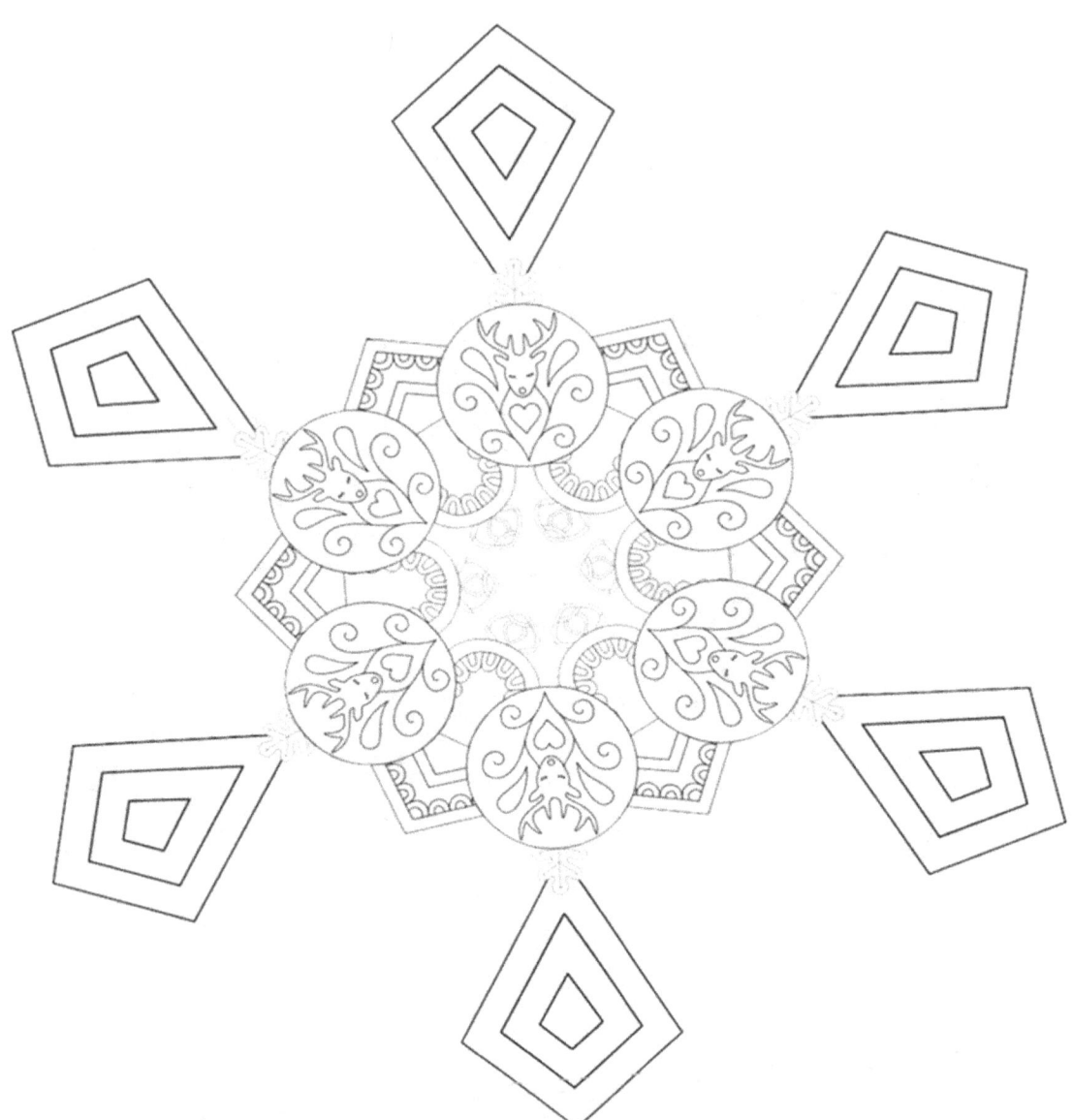

"The little may contrast with the great, in painting, but cannot be said to be contrary to it. Oppositions of colors contrast; but there are also colors contrary to each other, that is, which produce an ill effect because they shock the eye when brought very near it."
– Voltaire

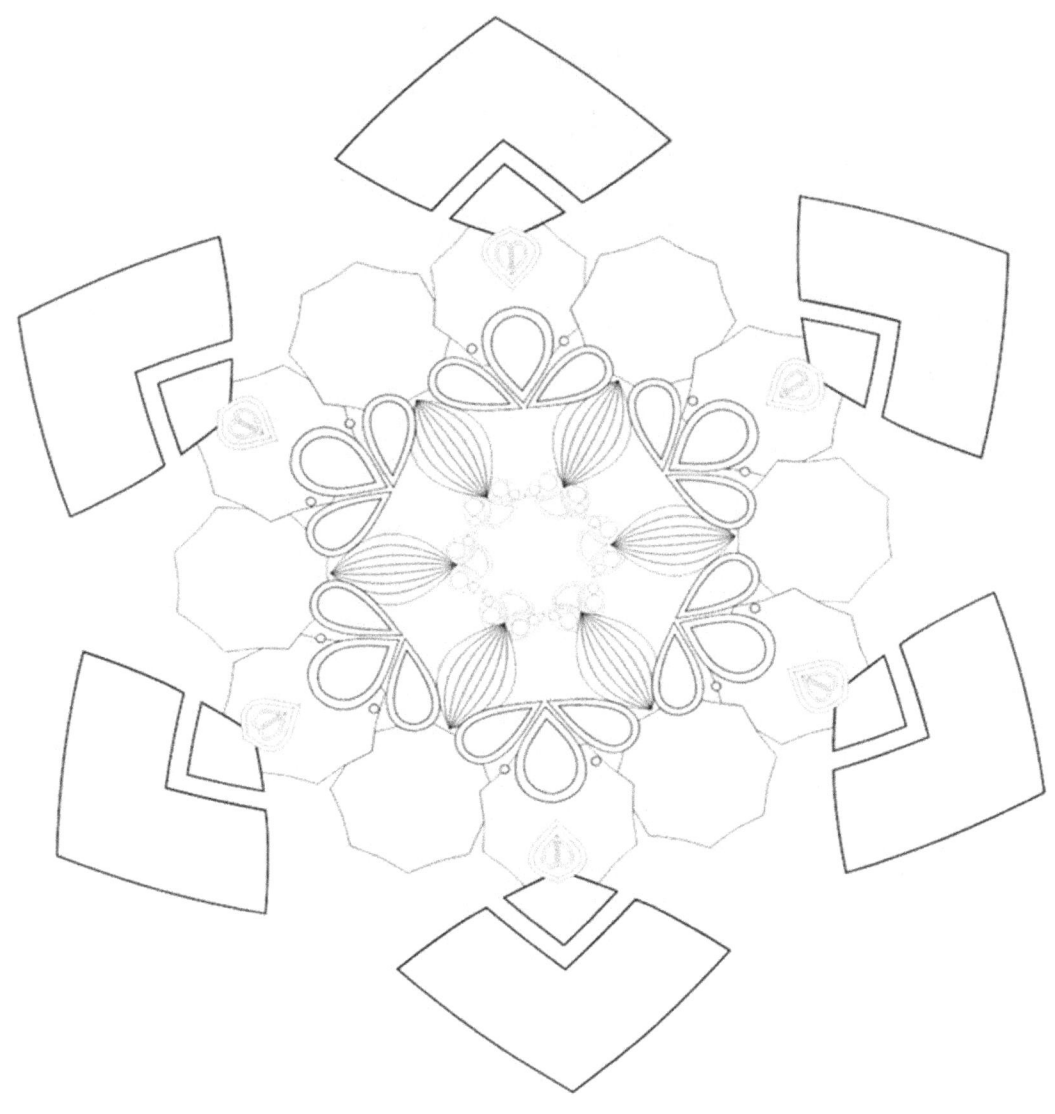

"You make different colors by combining those colors that already exist."
— Herbie Hancock

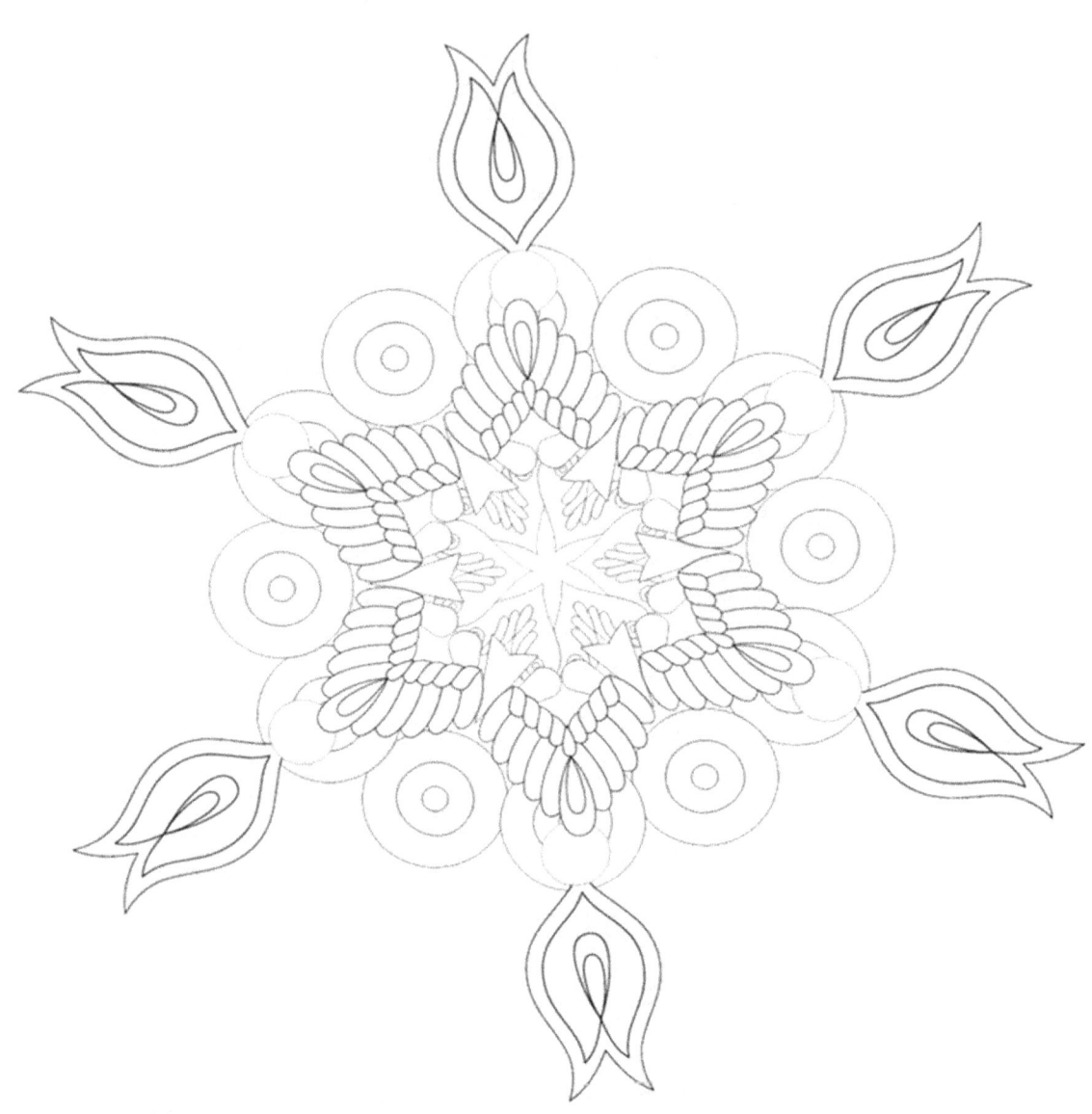

"Each color is applied to the canvas in relation to the colors next to it. The painting becomes a living thing and calls out for the color it wants."
– Neil Patterson

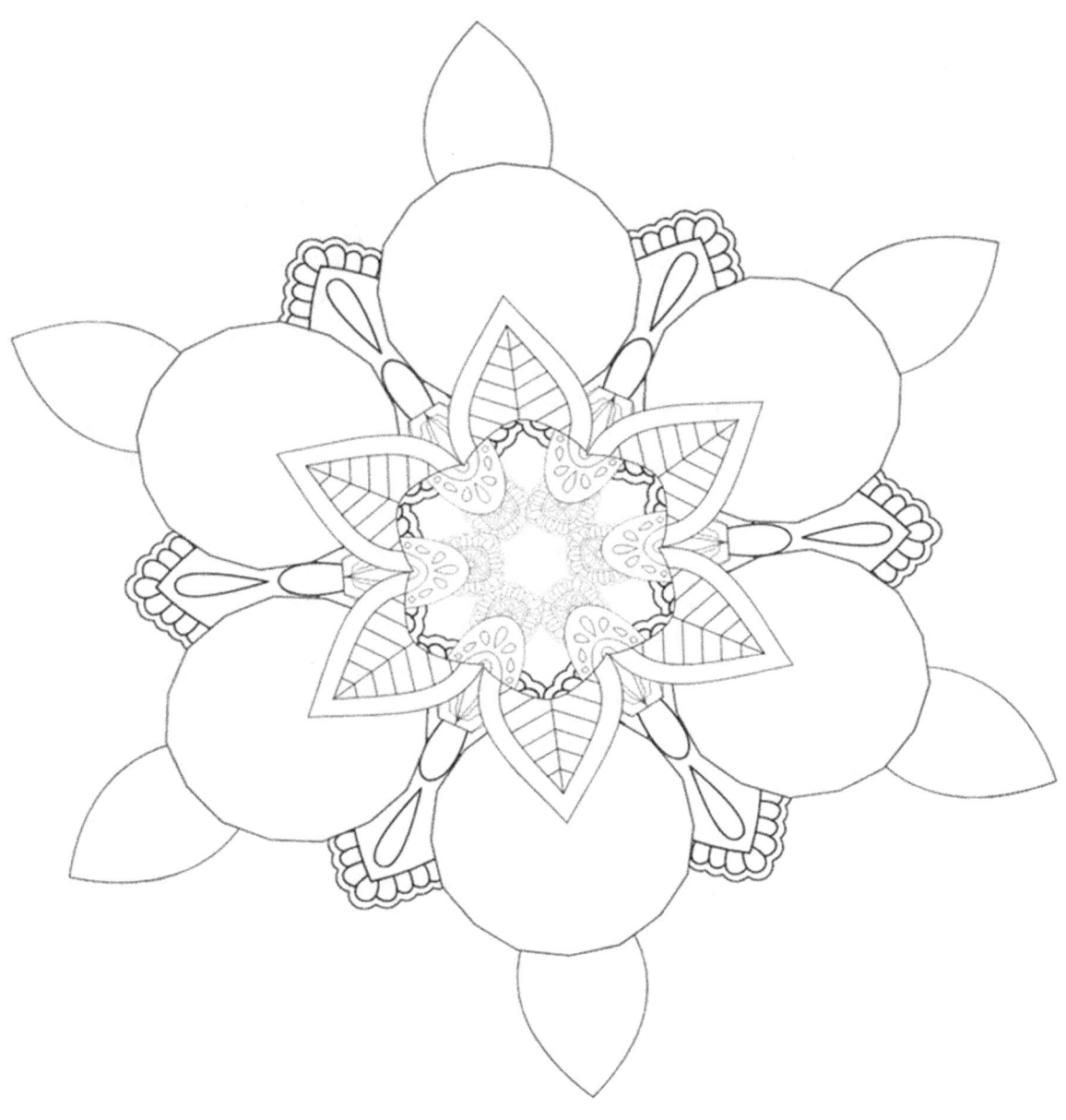

"When the color achieves richness, the form attains its fullness also."
– Paul Cezanne

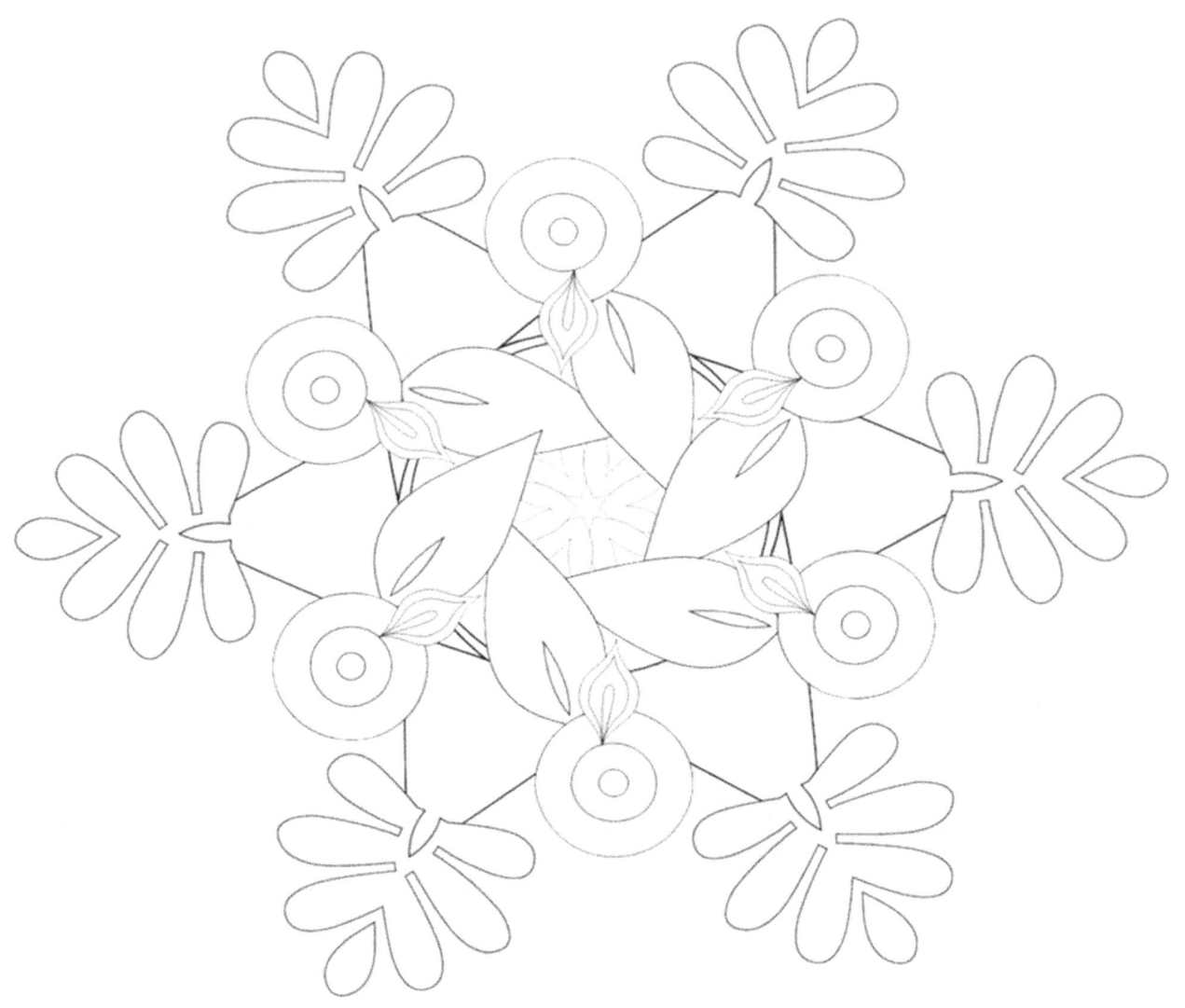

"The more an object is polished or brilliant, the less you see its own color and the more it becomes a mirror reflecting the color of its surroundings."
– Eugene Delacroix

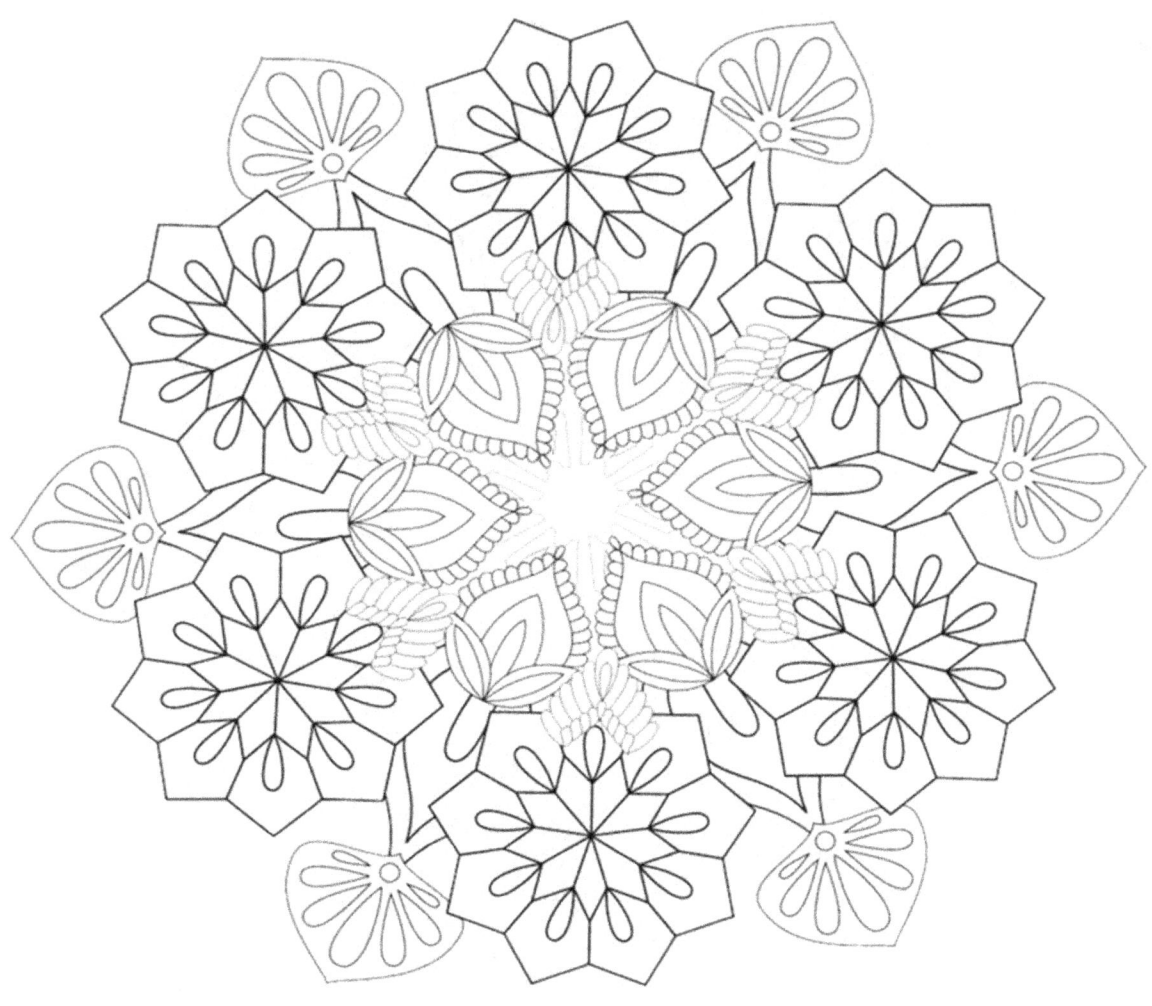

"Color could give rise to sensations
which would interfere with
our conception of space."
– Georges Braque

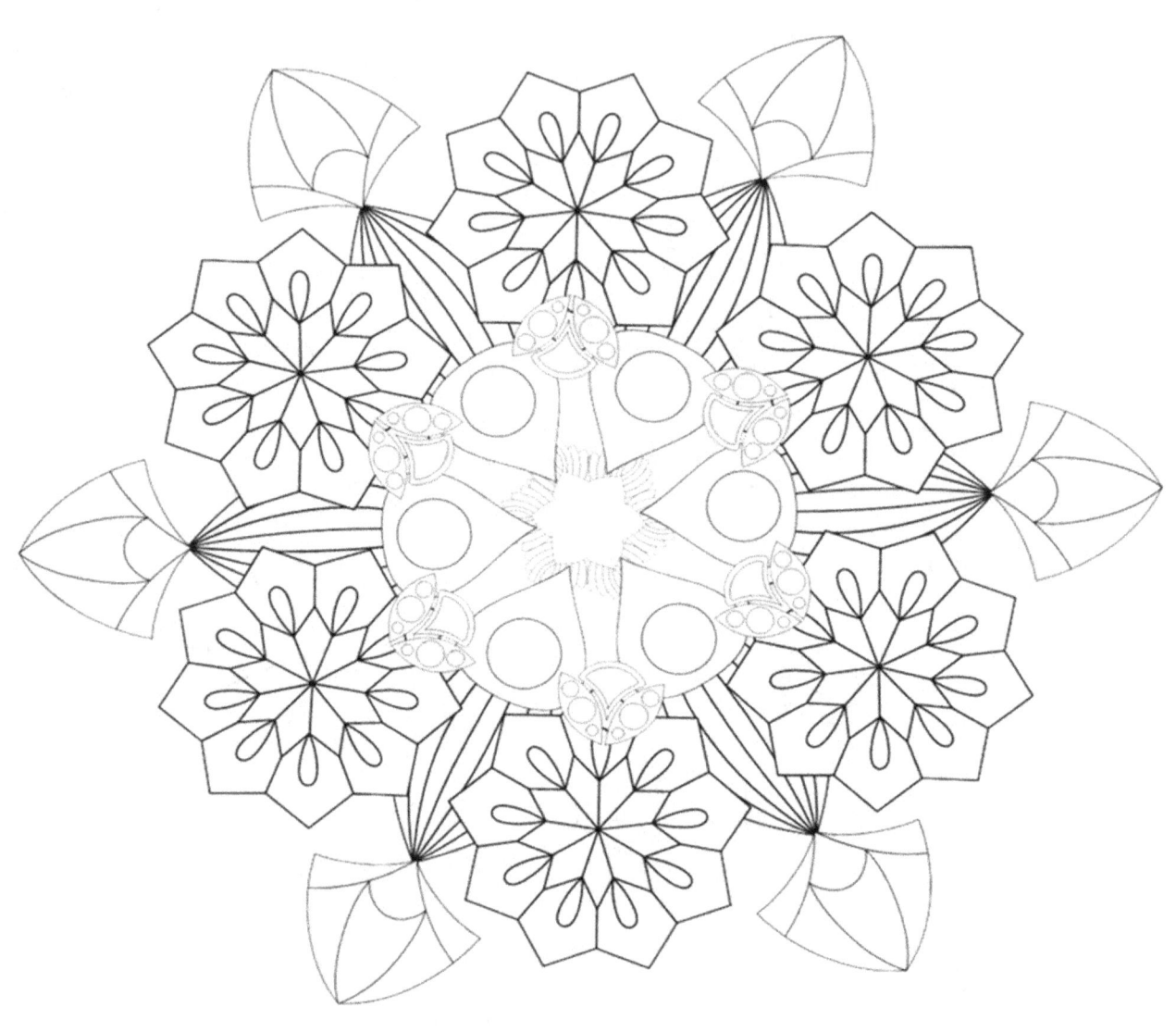

"The rhythm of relations of color and size makes the absolute appear in the relativity of time and space."
– Piet Mondrian

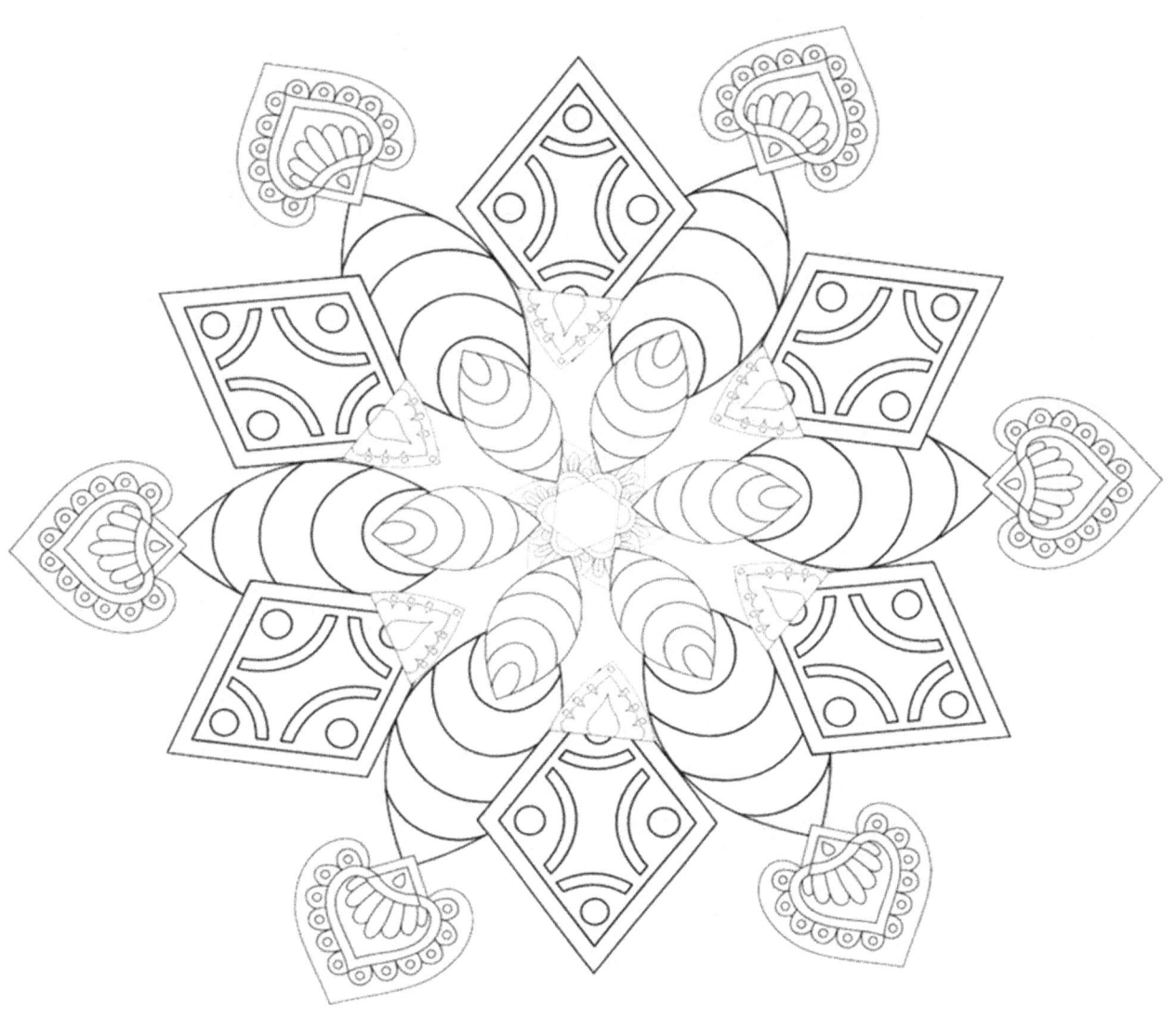

"Beauty without color
seems somehow to
belong to another world."
– Murasaki Shikibu

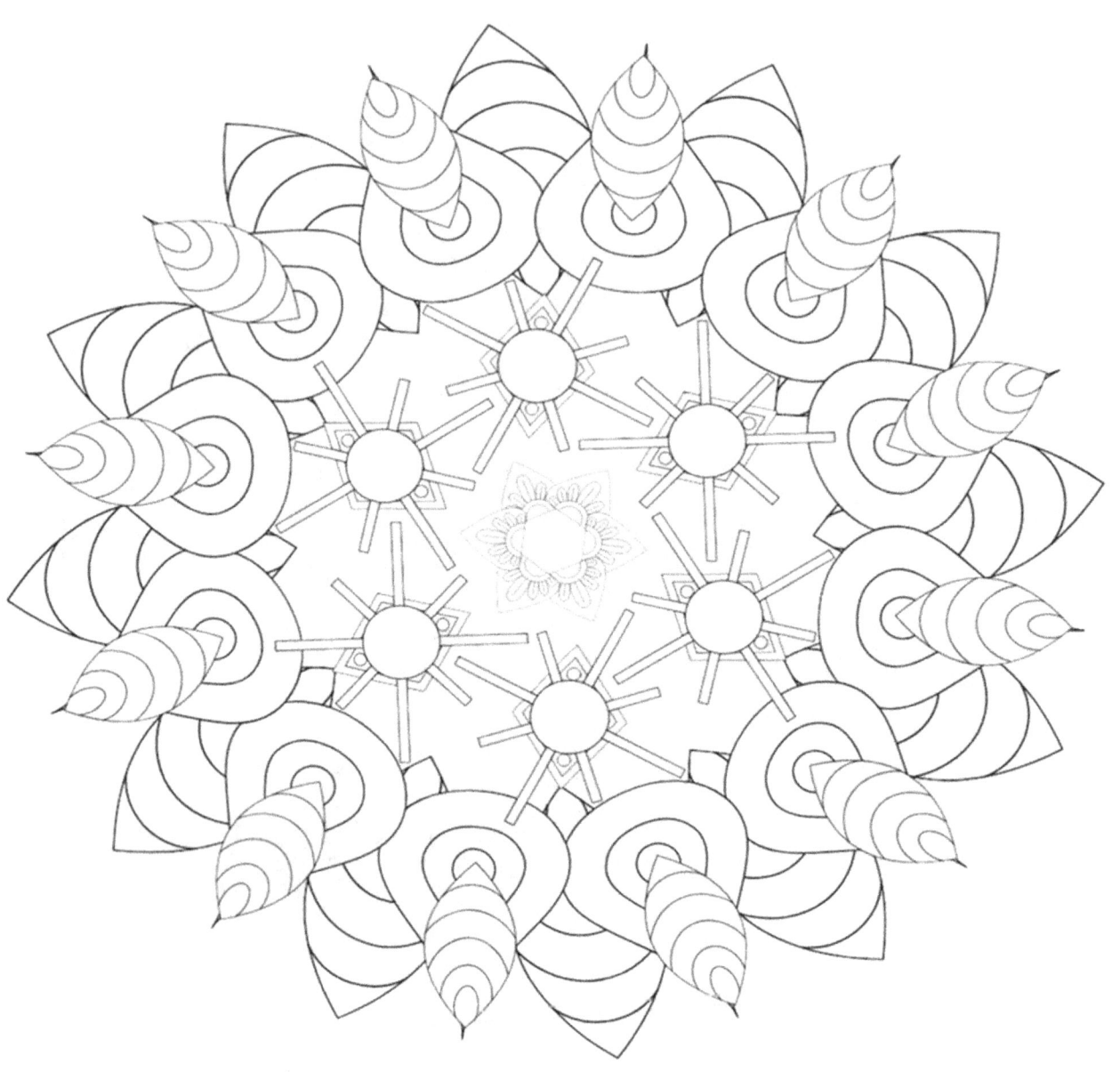

"Suffice it to say that black and white are also colors... for their simultaneous contrast is as striking as that of green and red, for instance."
– Vincent van Gogh

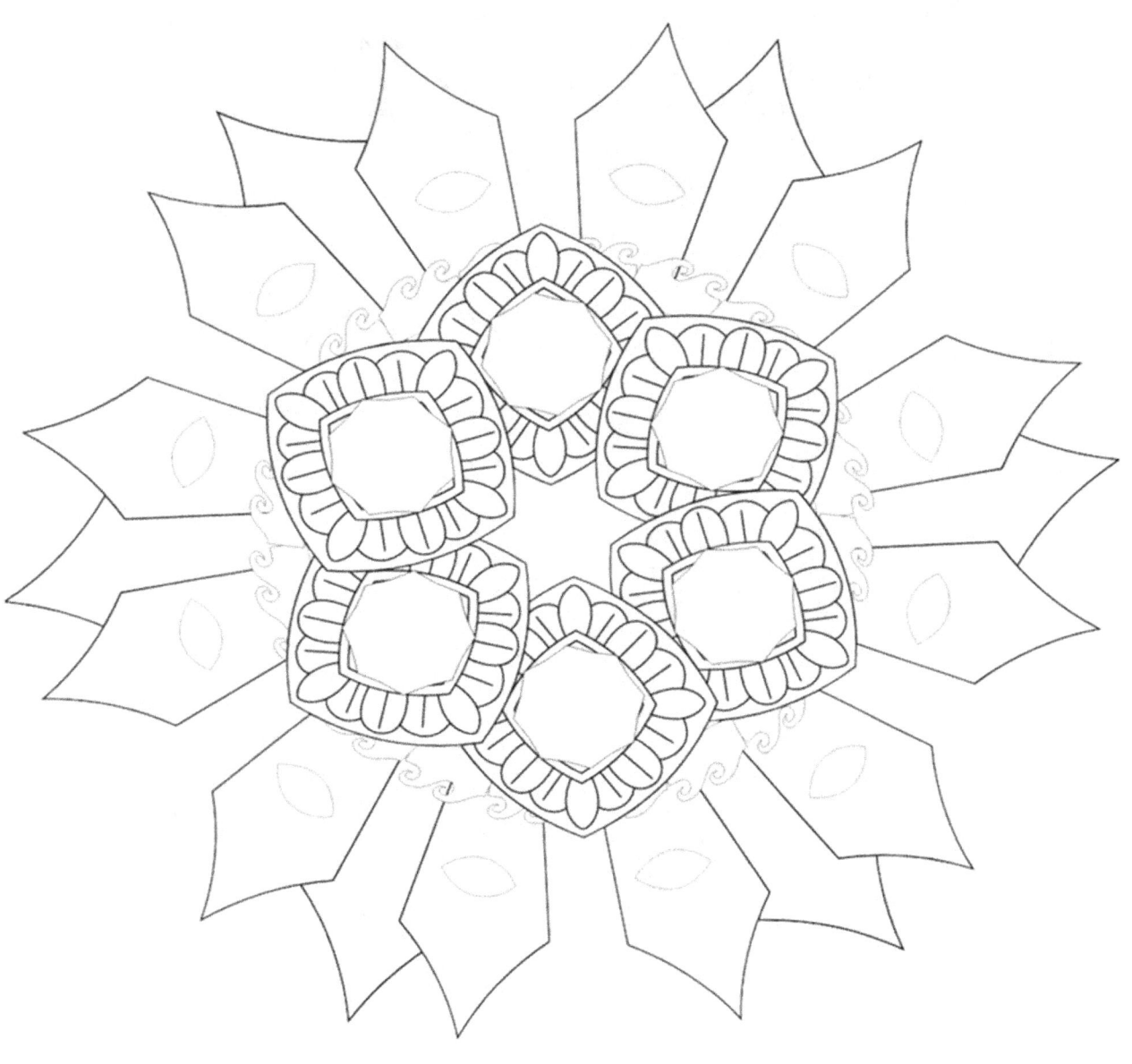

"Black and white is abstract; color is not.
Looking at a black and white photograph,
you are already looking at a strange world."
– Joel Sternfeld

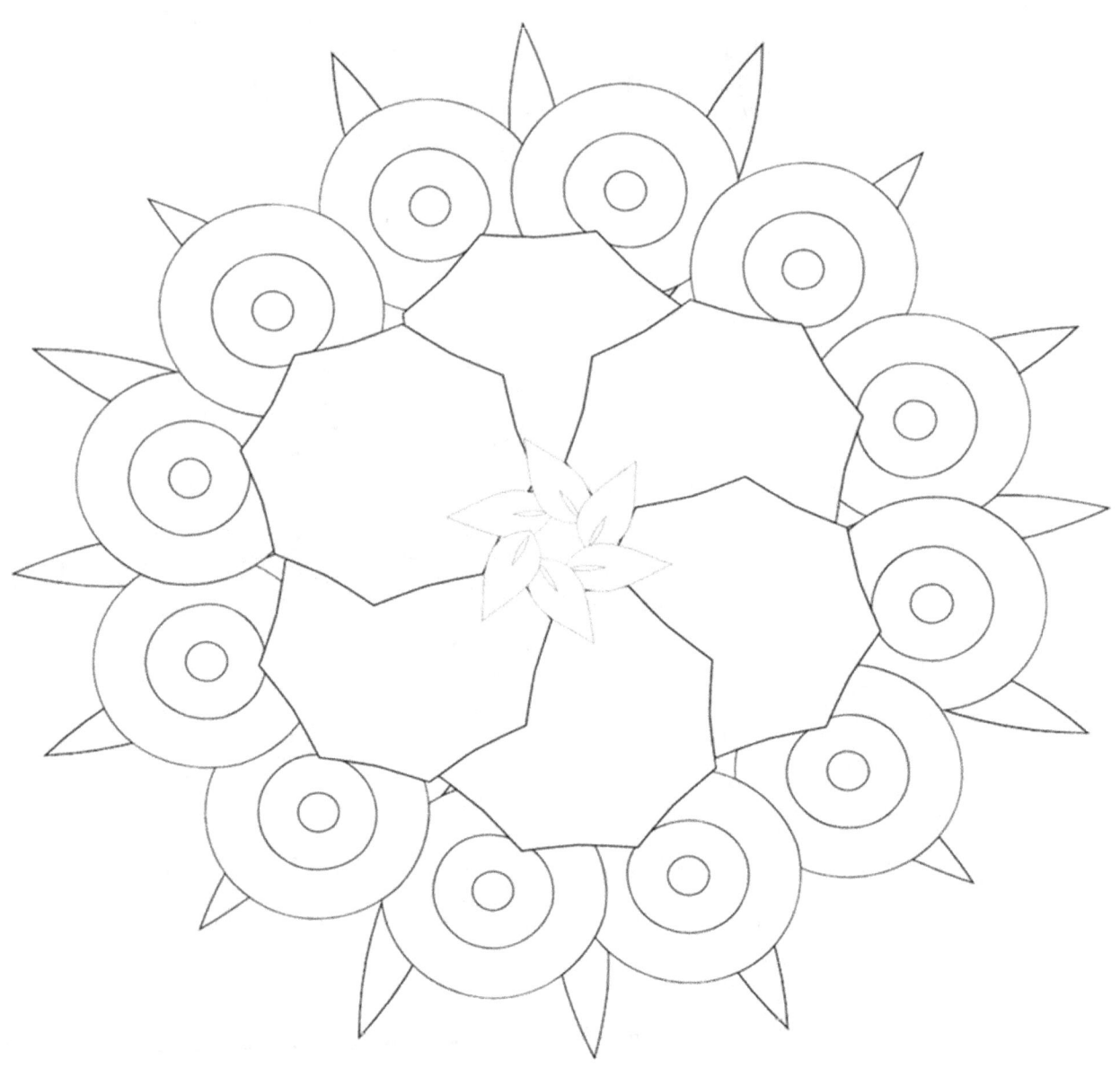

"White is not a mere absence of color; it is a shining and affirmative thing, as fierce as red, as definite as black. God paints in many colors; but He never paints so gorgeously, I had almost said so gaudily, as when He paints in white."
– G. K. Chesterton

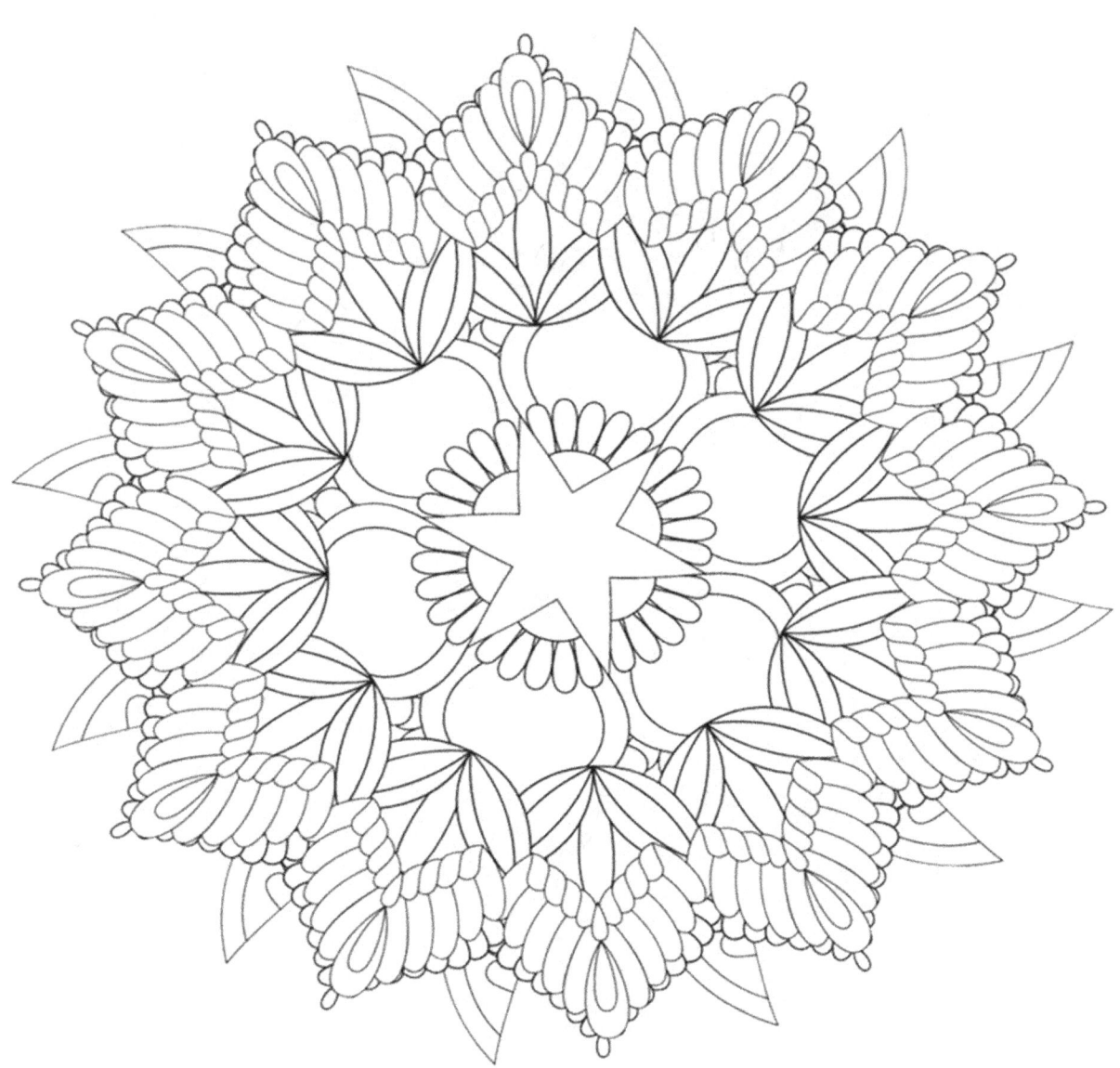

"Color is crucial in painting, but it is very hard to talk about. There is almost nothing you can say that holds up as a generalization, because it depends on too many factors: size, modulation, the rest of the field, a certain consistency that color has with forms, and the statement you're trying to make."
– Roy Lichtenstein

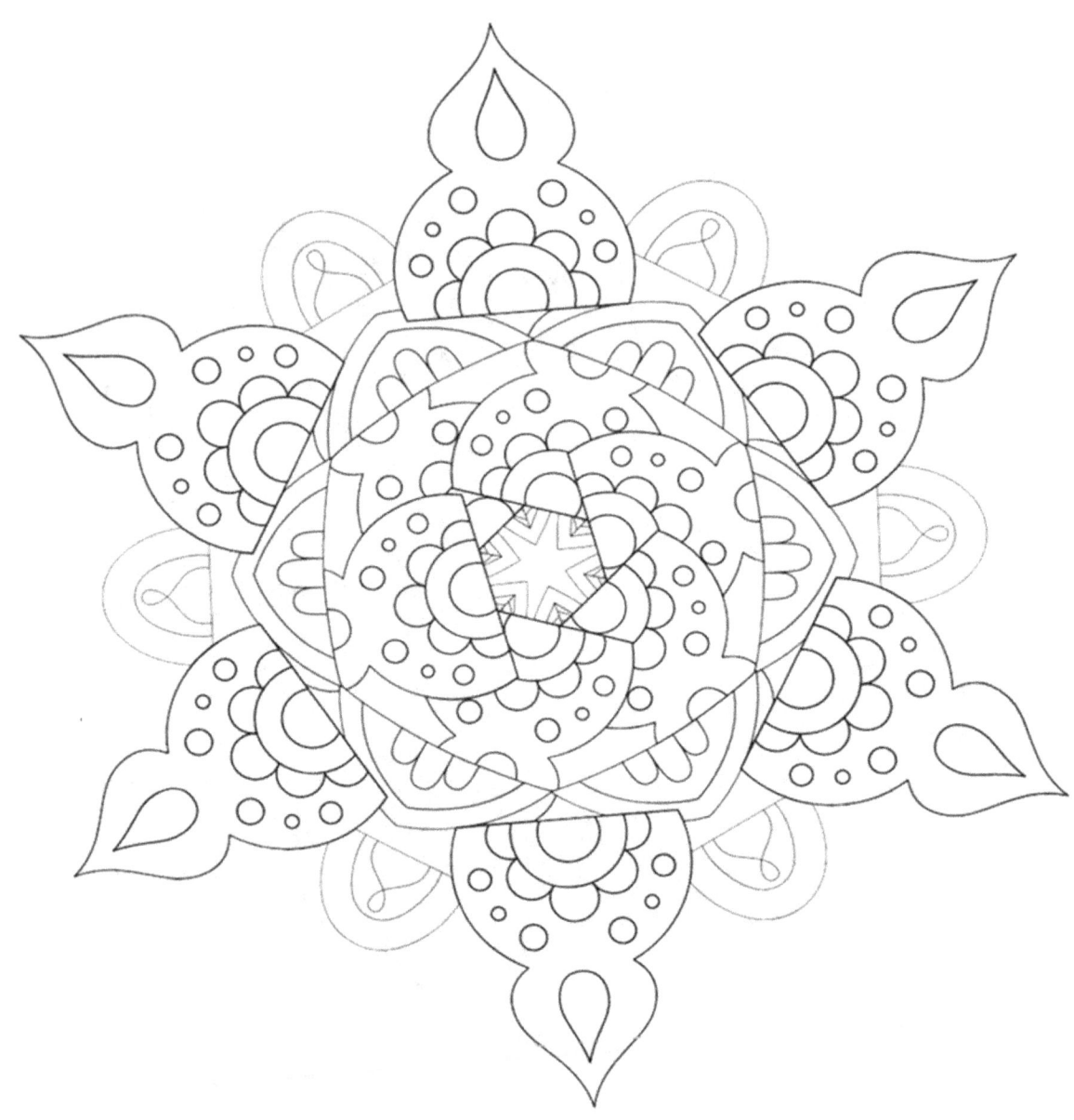

"If one says 'red' – the name of color –
and there are fifty people listening,
it can be expected that there will be
fifty reds in their minds. And one can be
sure that all these reds will be very different."
– Josef Albers

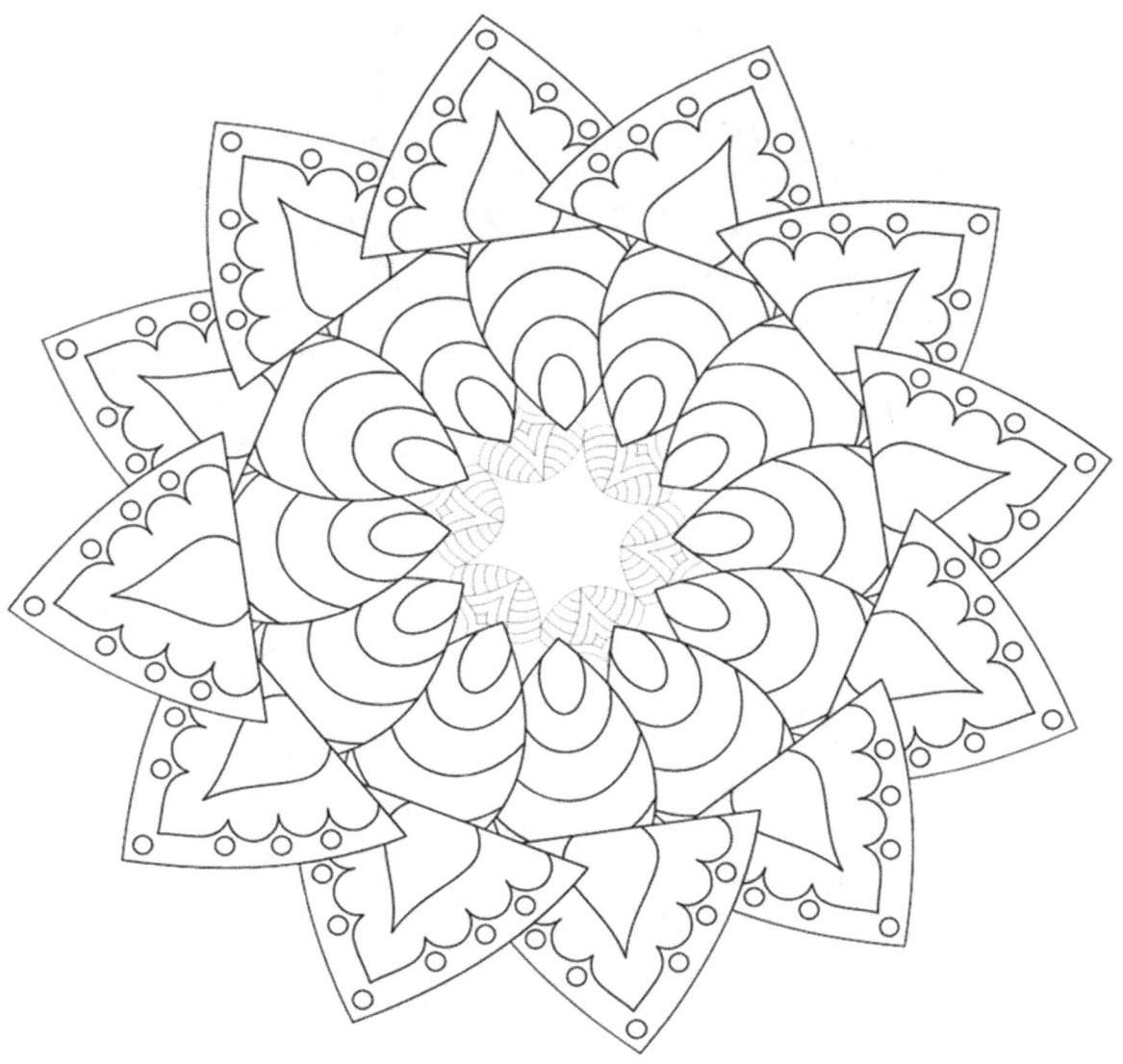

"Color is uncontainable. It effortlessly reveals the limits of language and evades our best attempts to impose a rational order on it... To work with color is to become acutely aware of the insufficiency of language and theory – which is both disturbing and pleasurable."
– David Batchelor

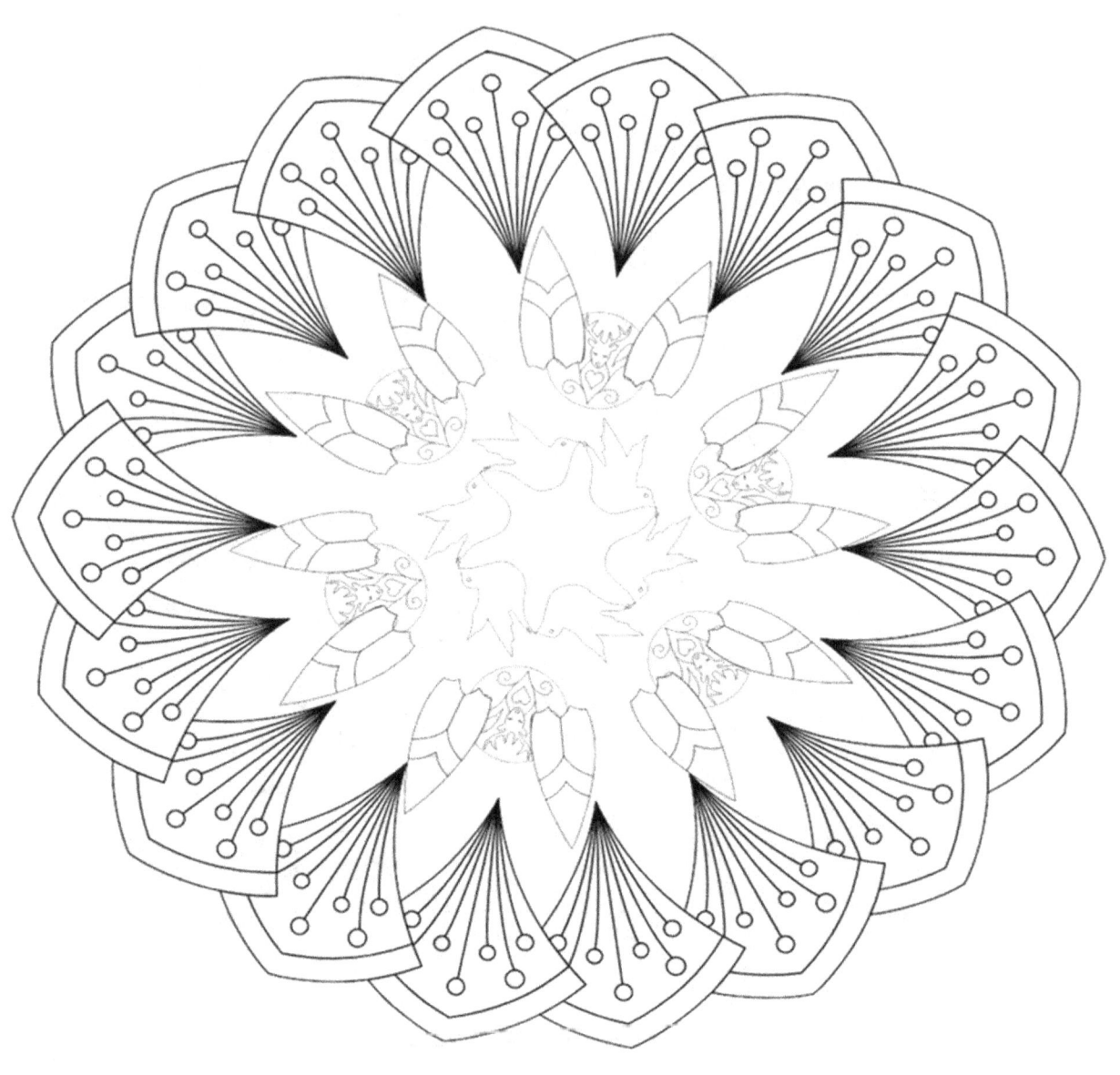

"I found I could say things with colors that I couldn't say in any other way — things that I had no words for."
— Georgia O'Keeffe

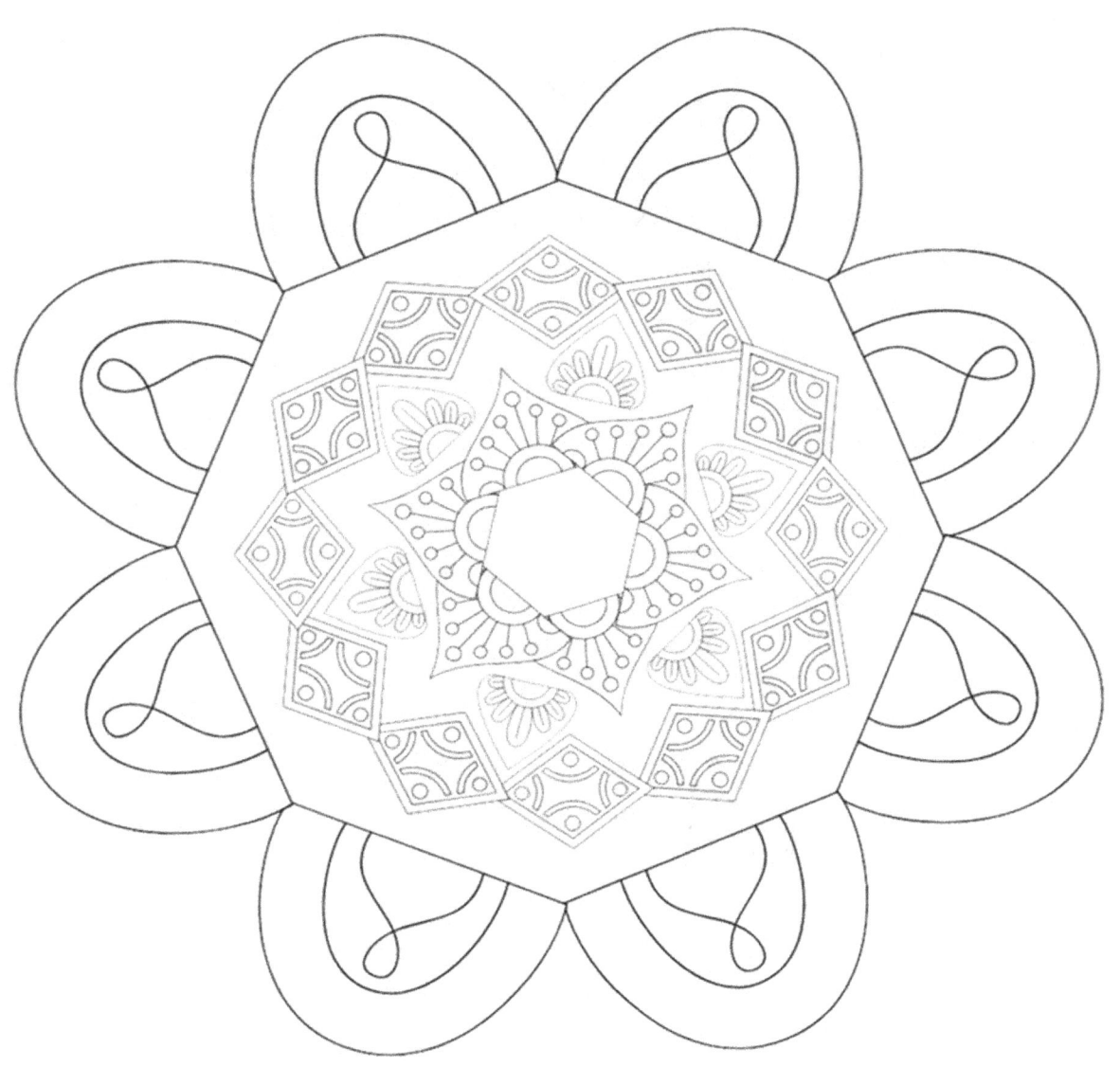

"Color is only
beautiful when it
means something."
– Robert Henri

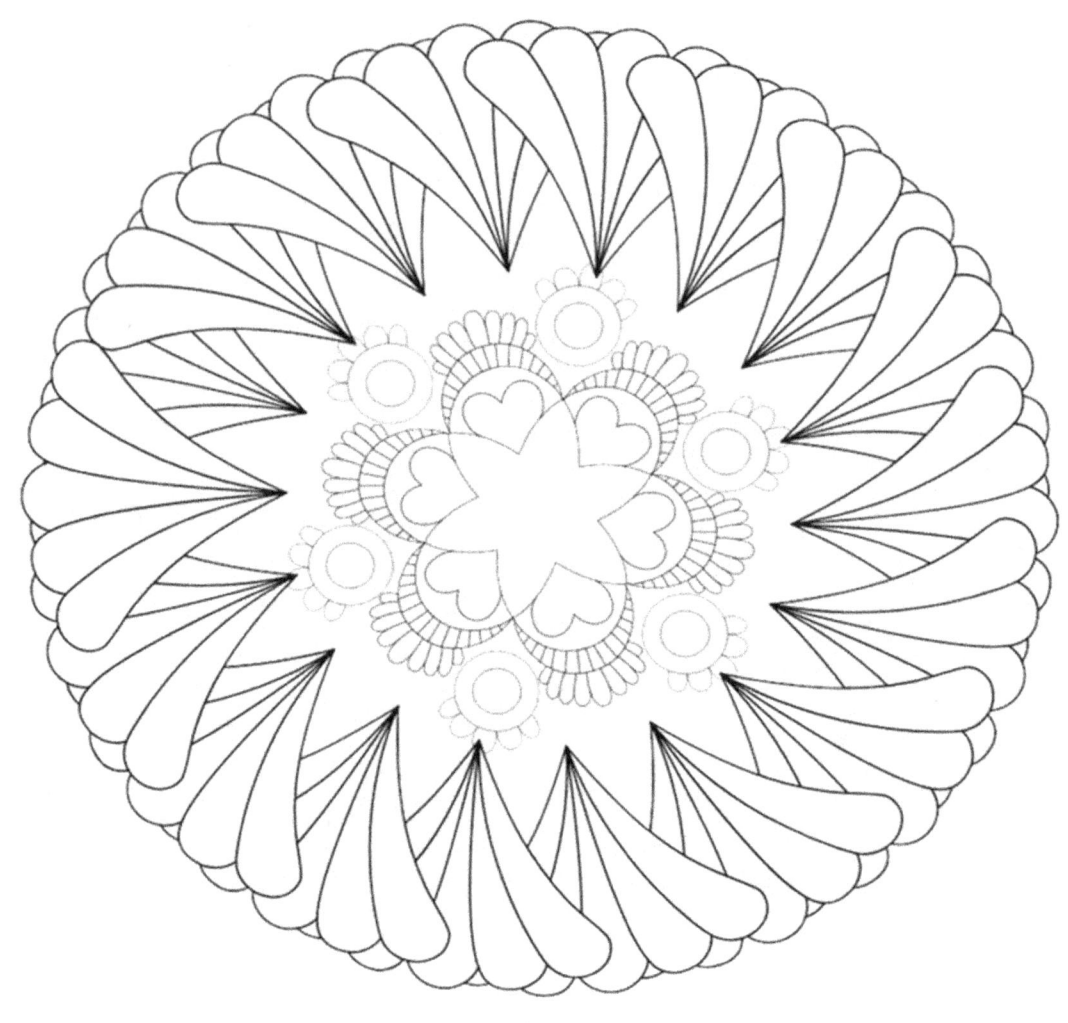

"Color does not add a pleasant quality to design – it reinforces it."
– Pierre Bonnard

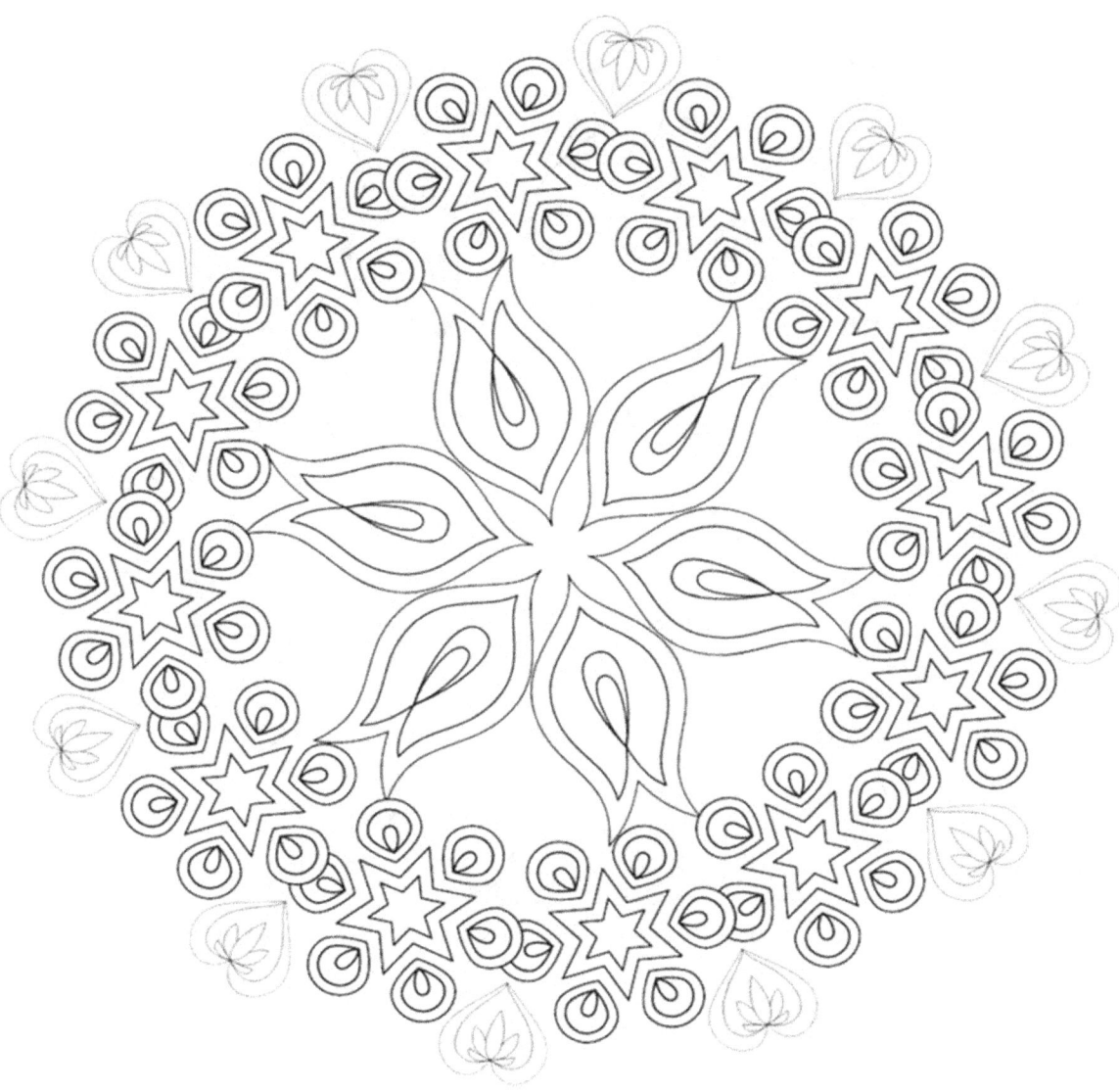

"Color can overwhelm... One must understand that when it comes to color, 'less' is often 'more' – lesson taught us by the masters but ignored by many artists."
– Joe Singer

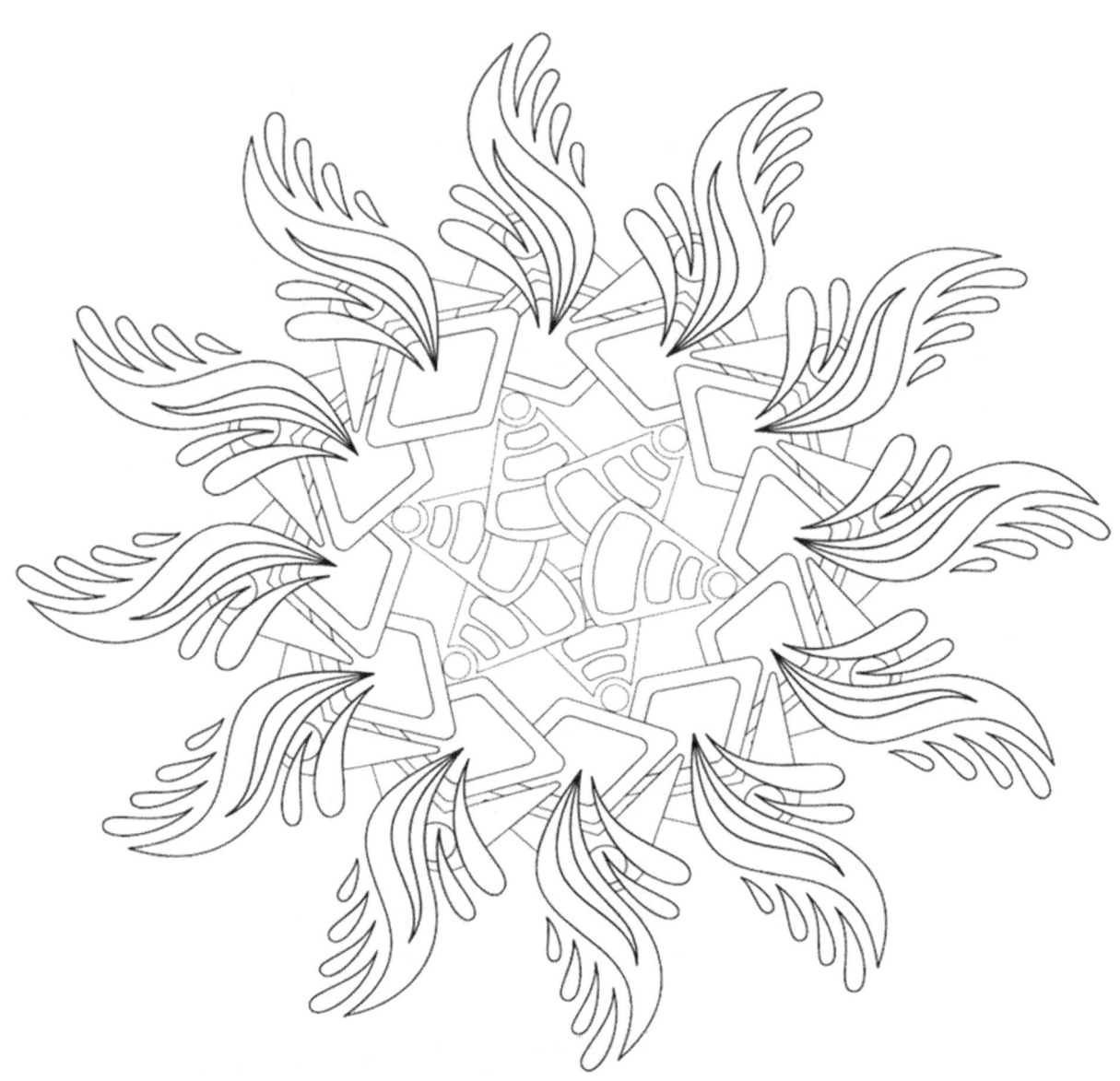

"I try to construct a picture in which shapes, spaces, colors, form a set of unique relationships, independent of any subject matter. At the same time I try to capture and translate the excitement and emotion aroused in me by the impact with the original idea."
– Milton Avery

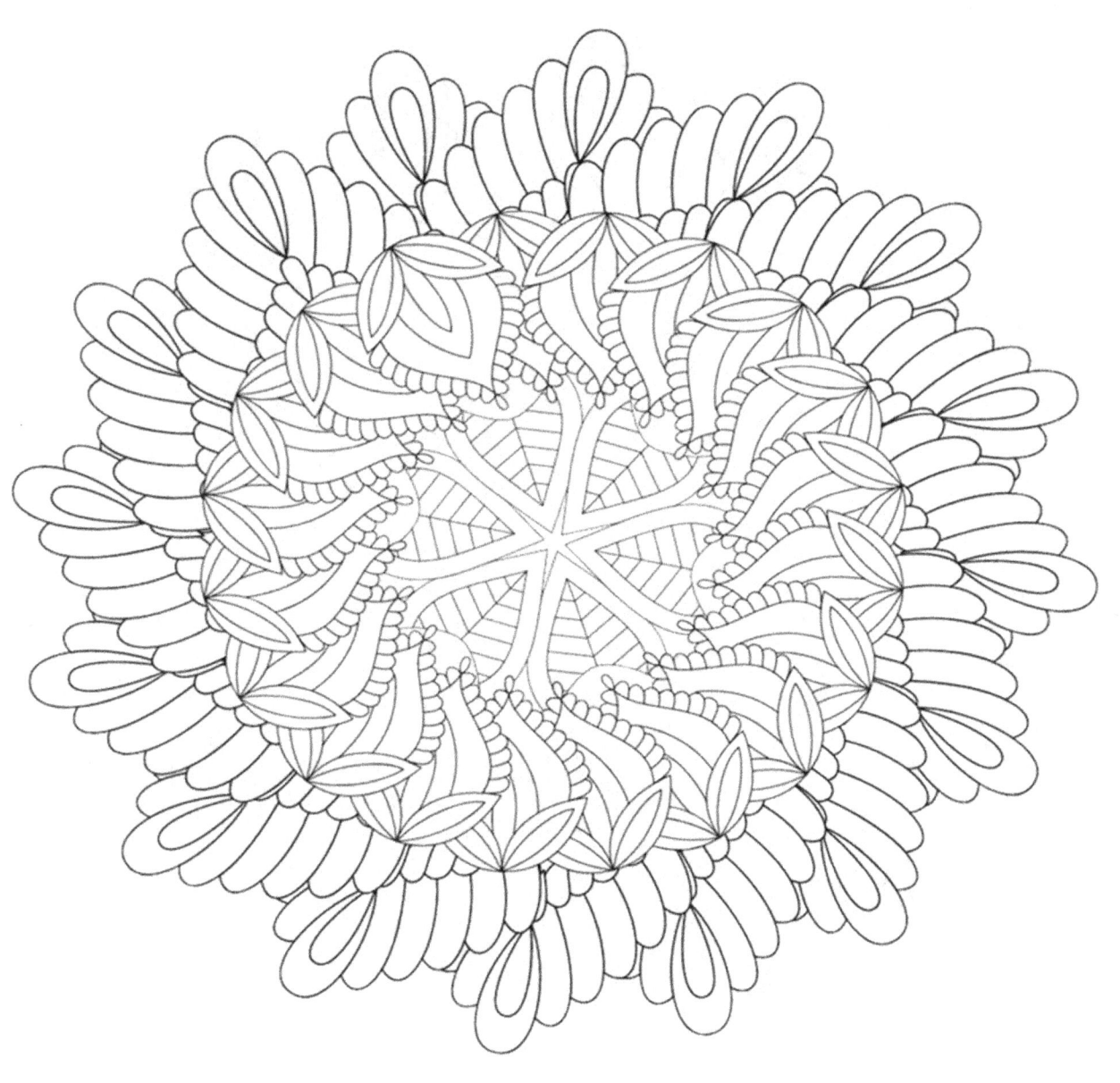

"You put down one color and it calls for an answer. You have to look at it like a melody."
– Romare Bearden

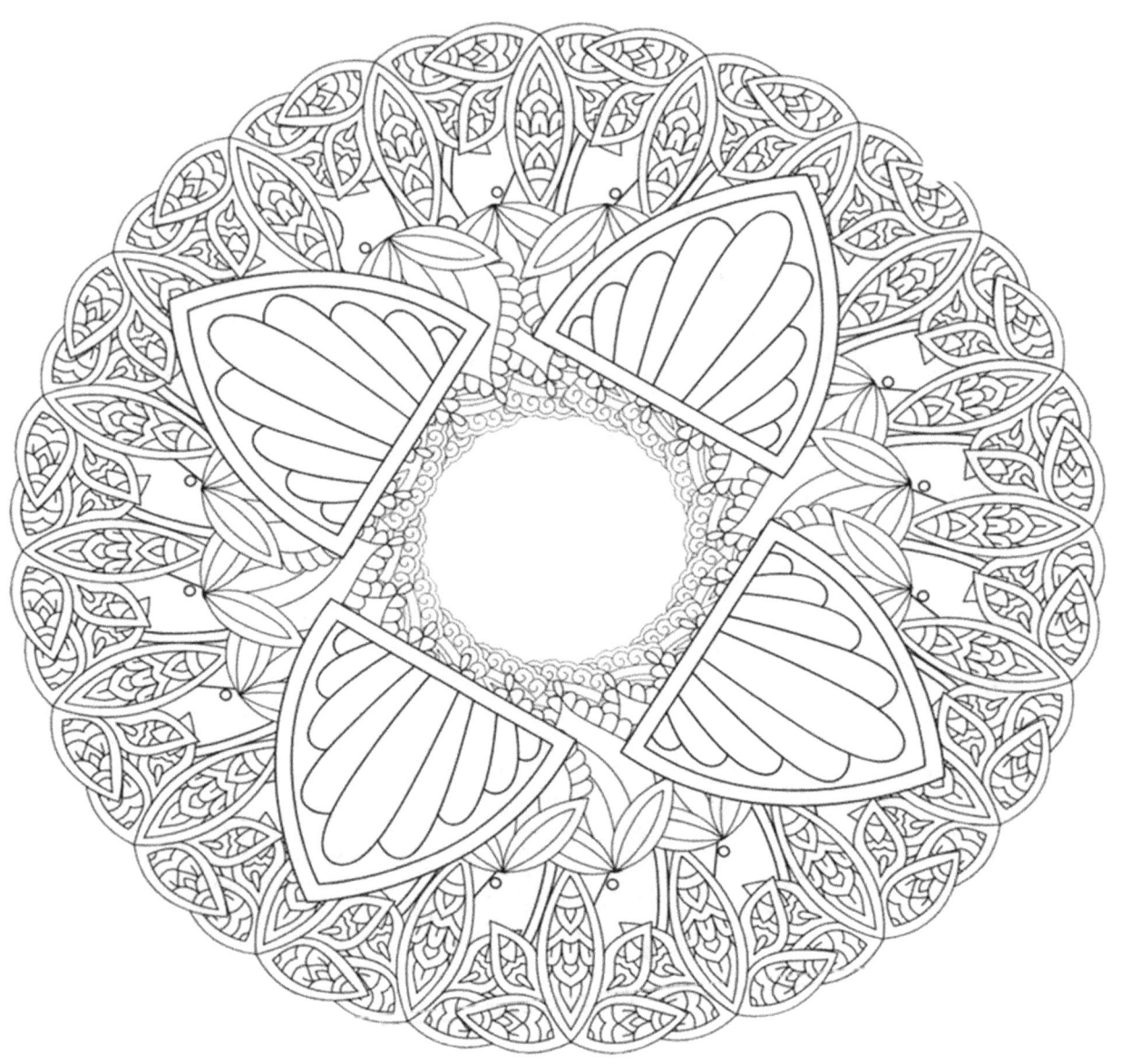

"Life is about using the whole box of crayons."
— RuPaul

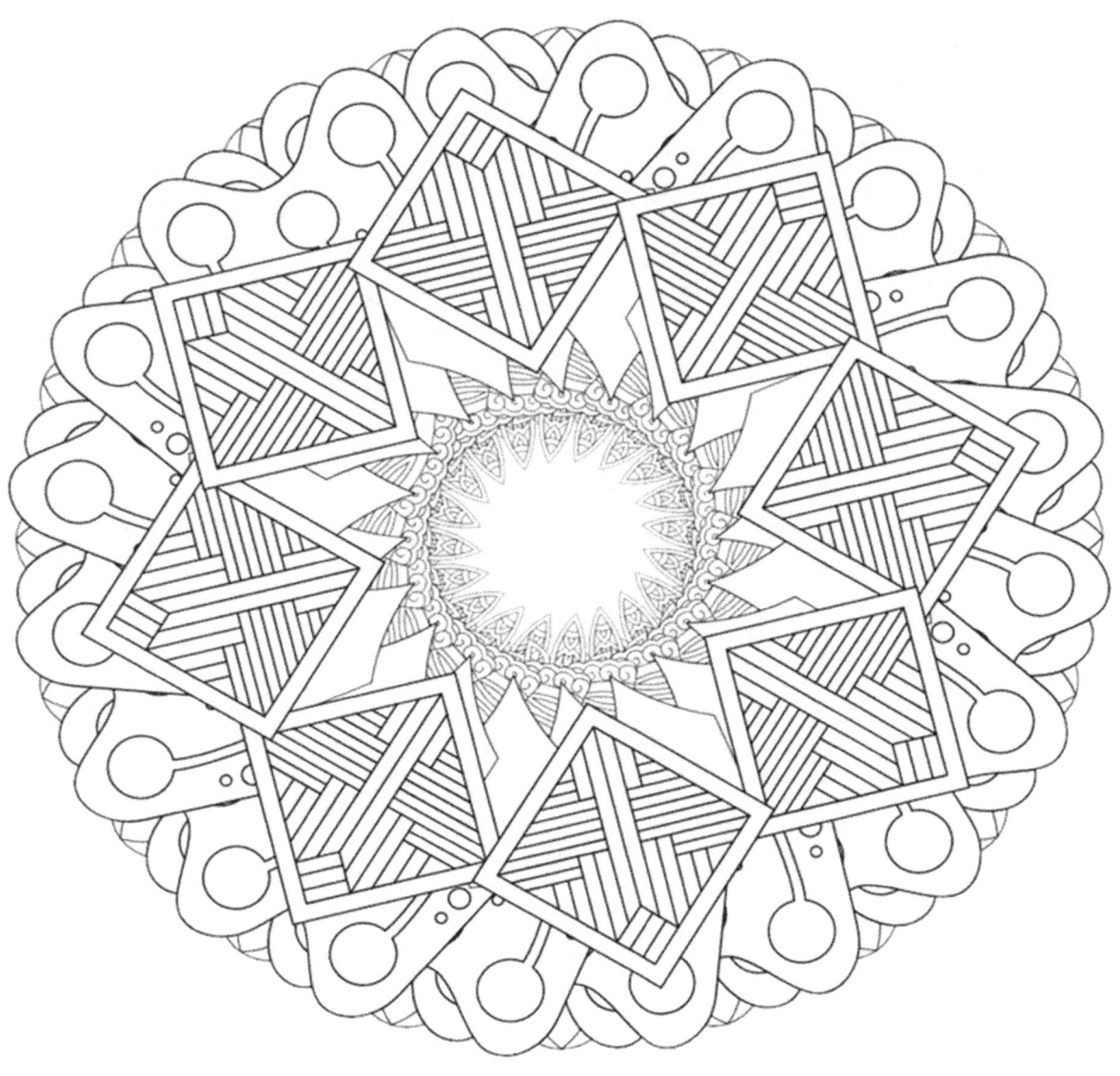

"Color is like cooking. The cook puts in more or less salt, that's the difference!"
– Josef Albers

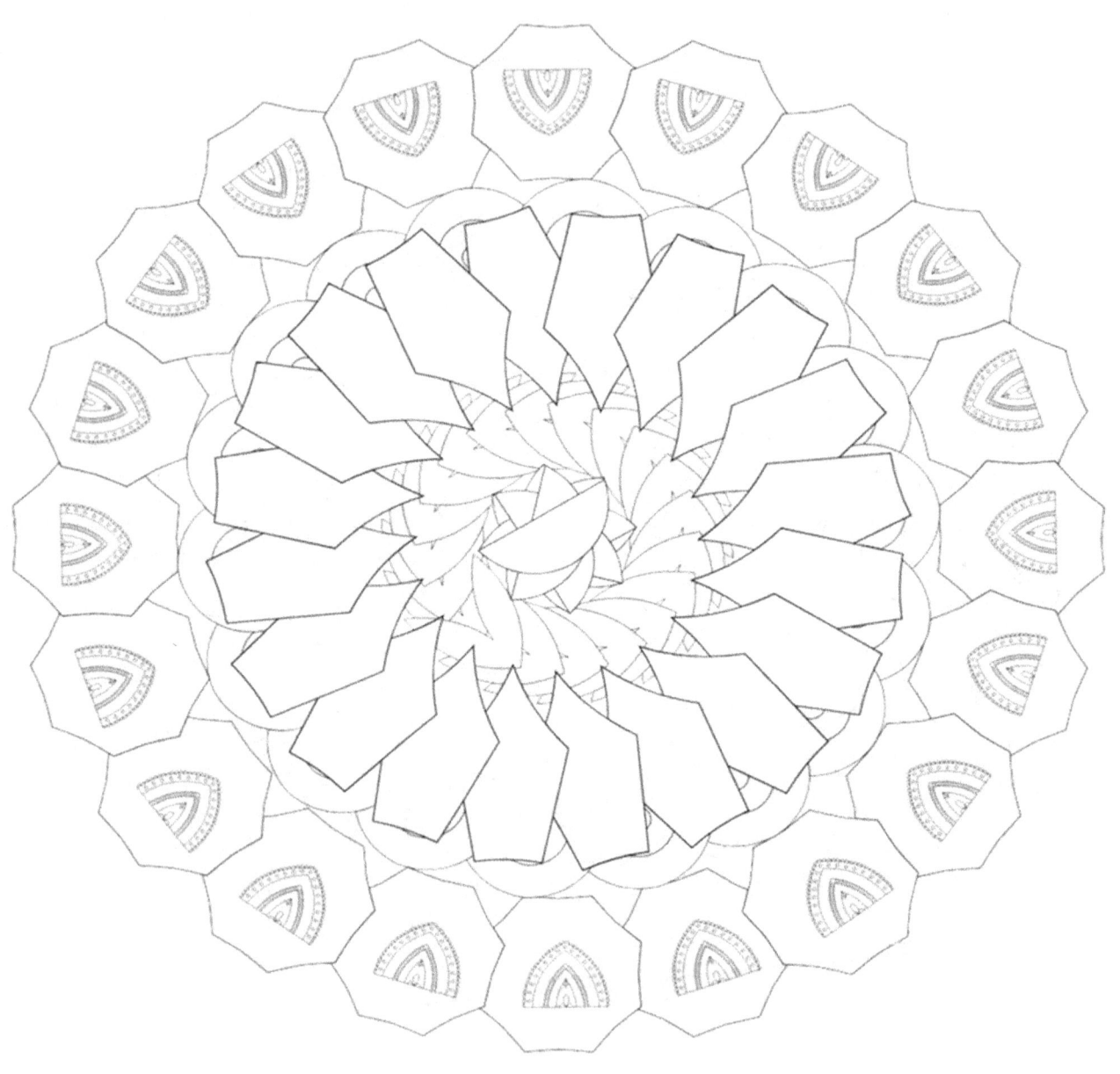

"I prefer living in color."
— David Hockney

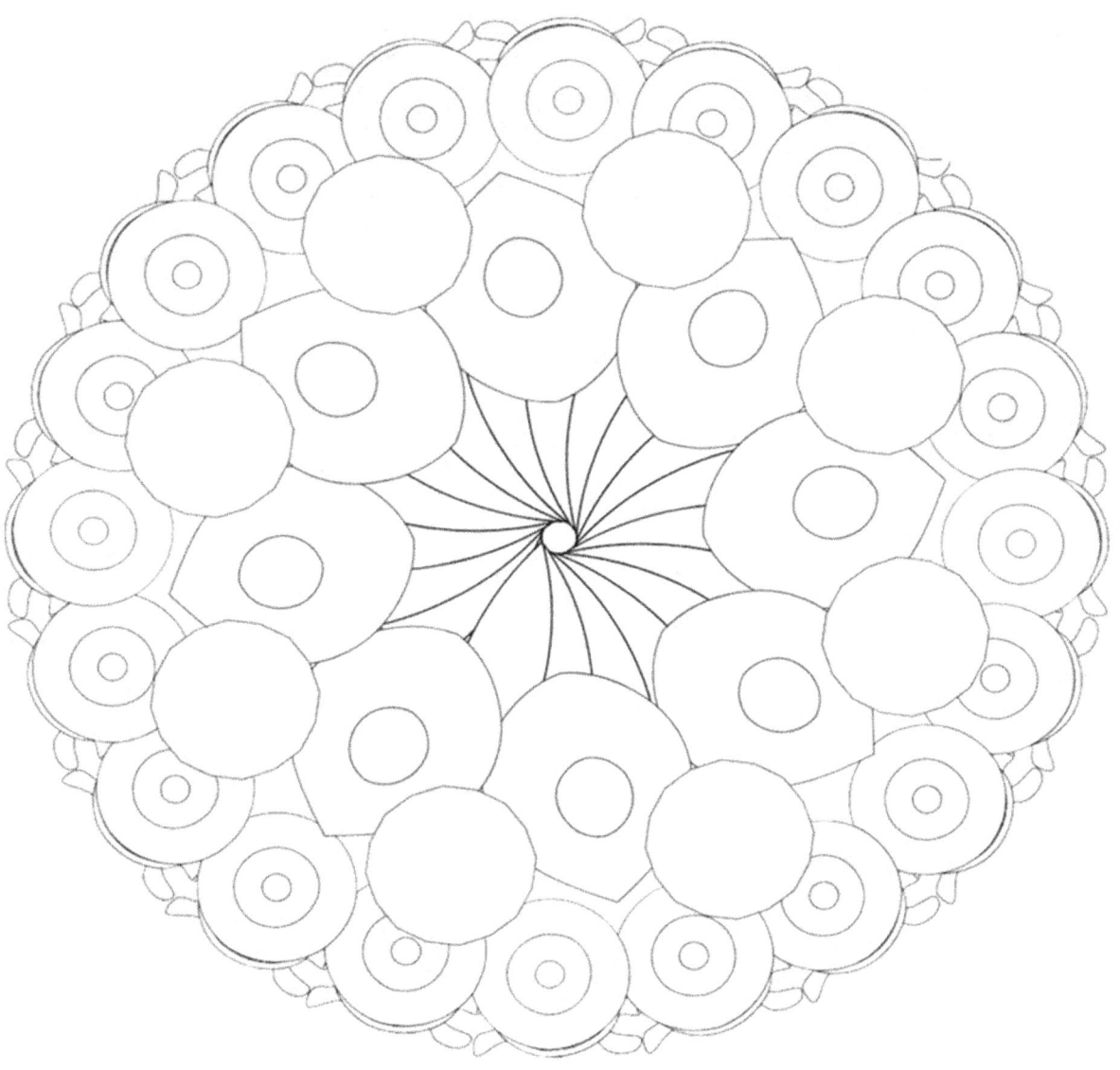

"The colors live a remarkable life
of their own after they have
been applied to the canvas."
– Edvard Munch

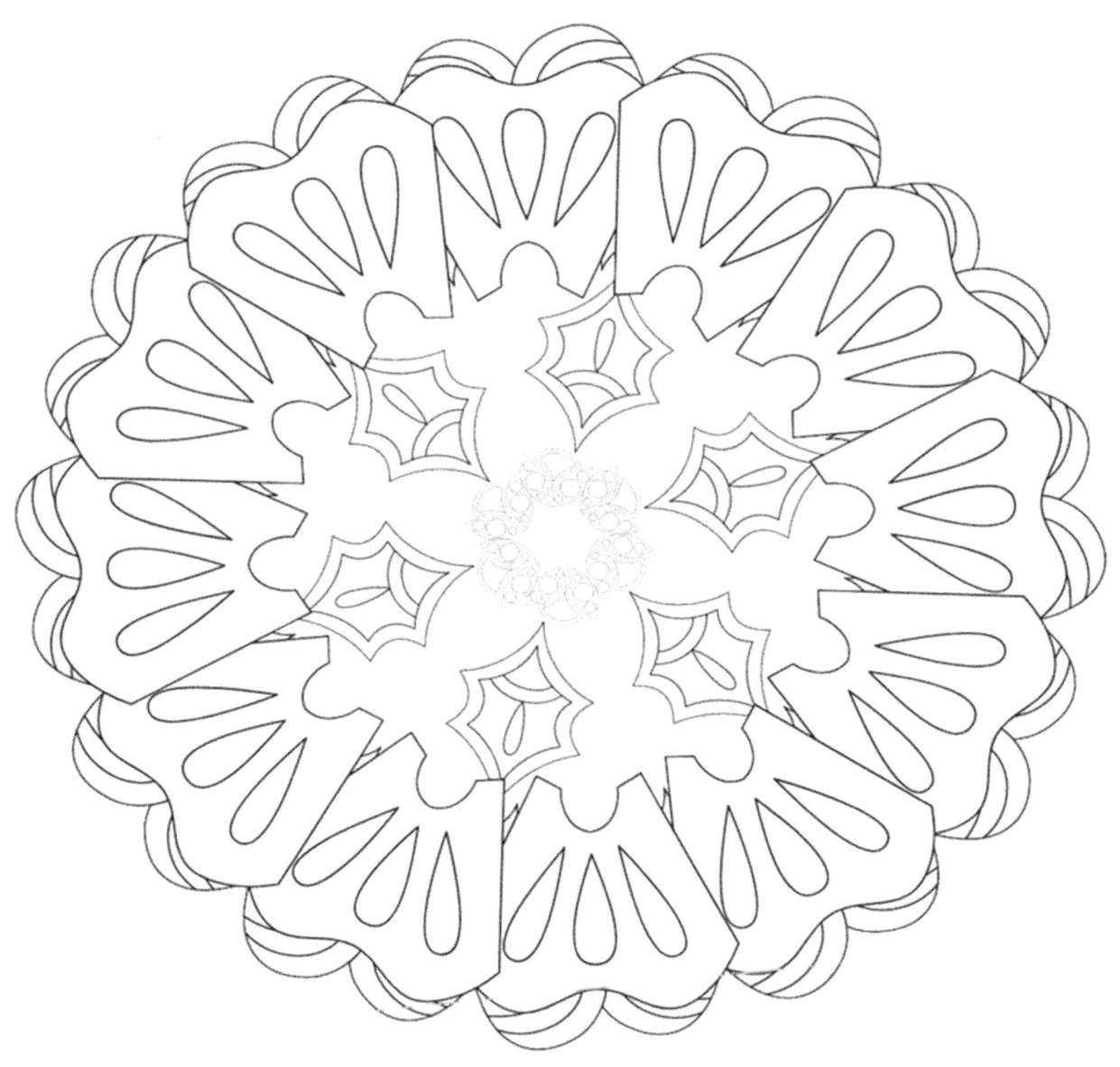

"Color... thinks by itself, independently of the object it clothes."
– Charles Baudelaire

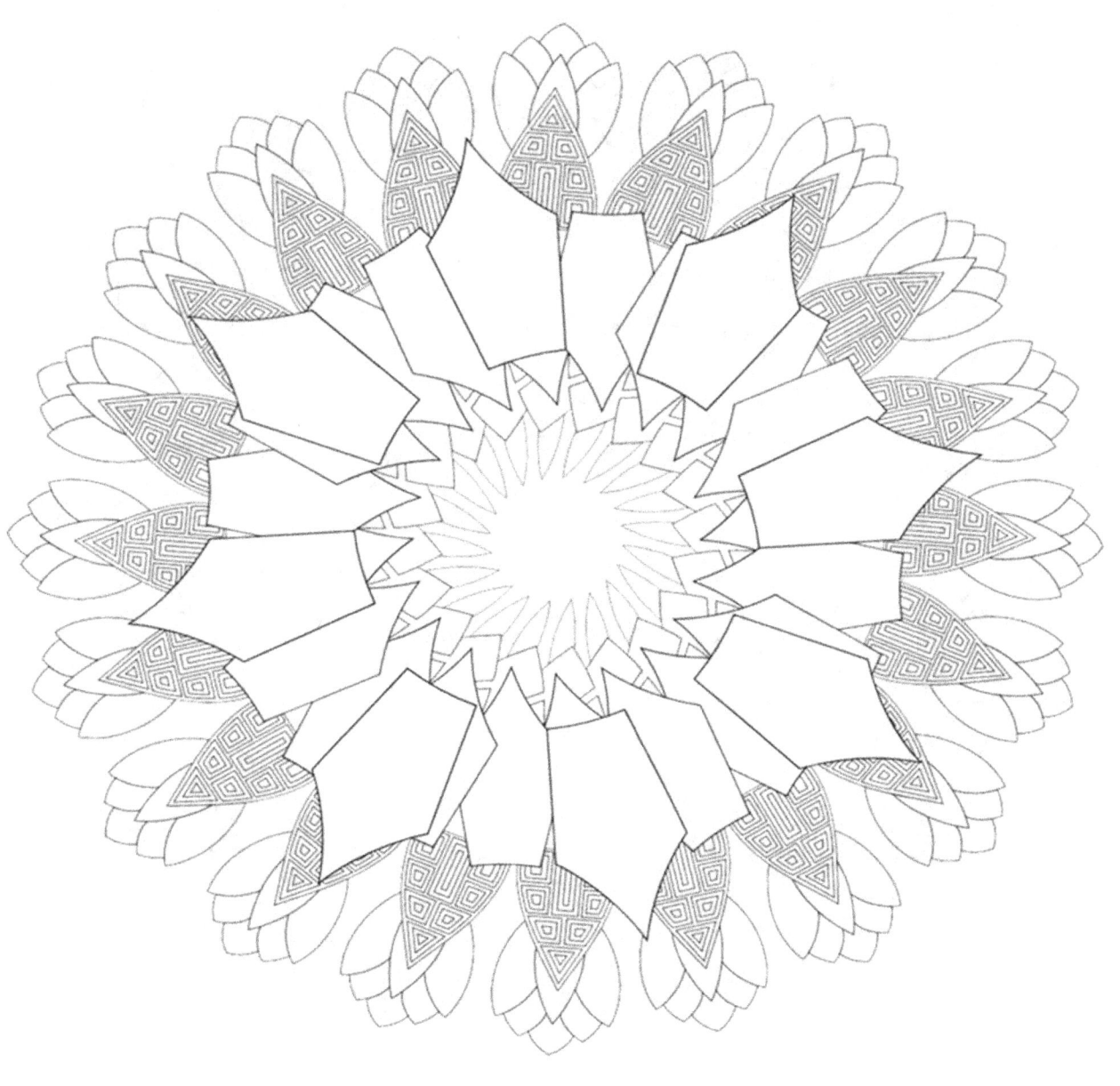

"I never met a color I didn't like."
– Dale Chihuly

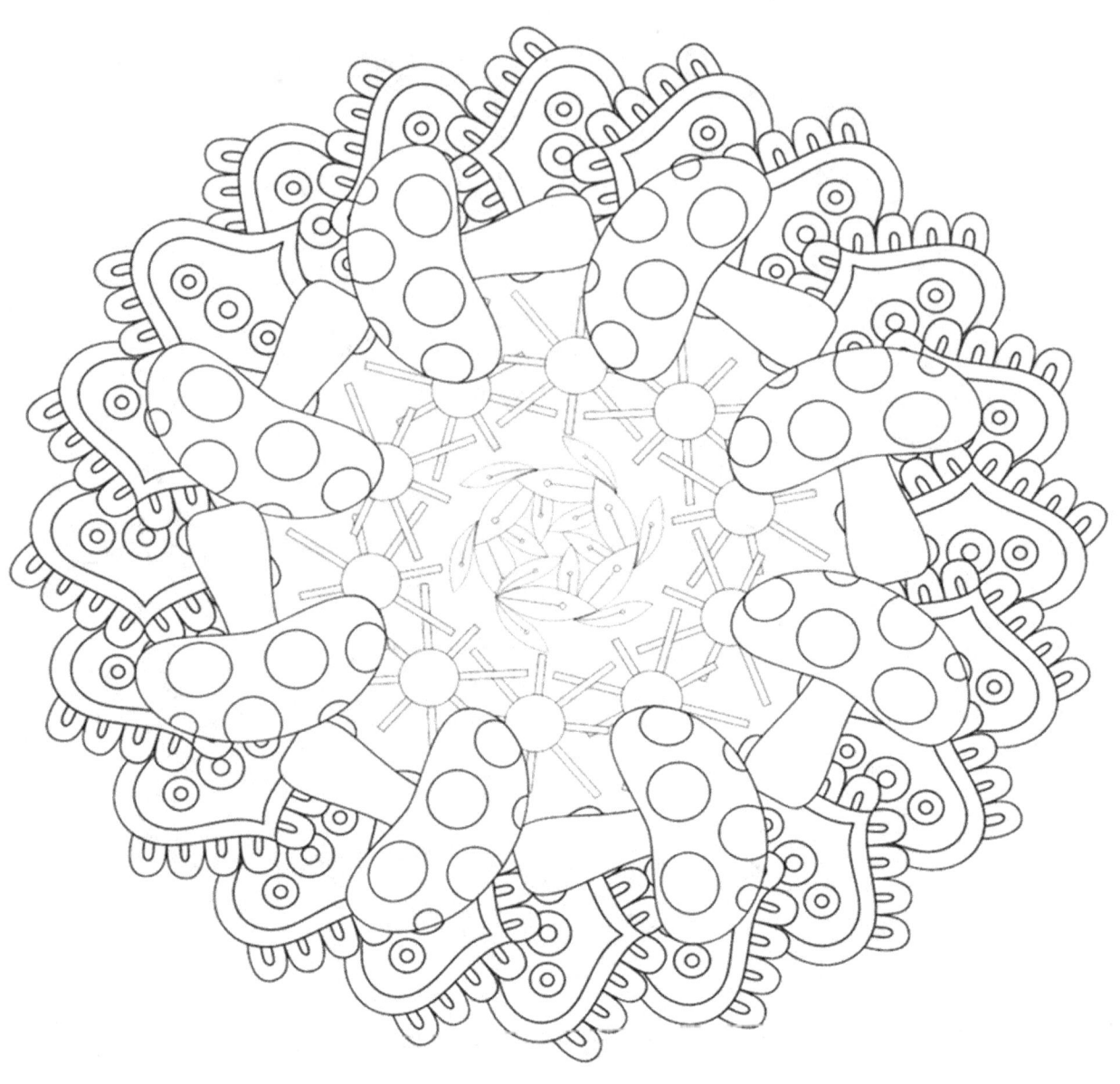

"And all the colors I am inside have not been invented yet."
– Shel Silverstein

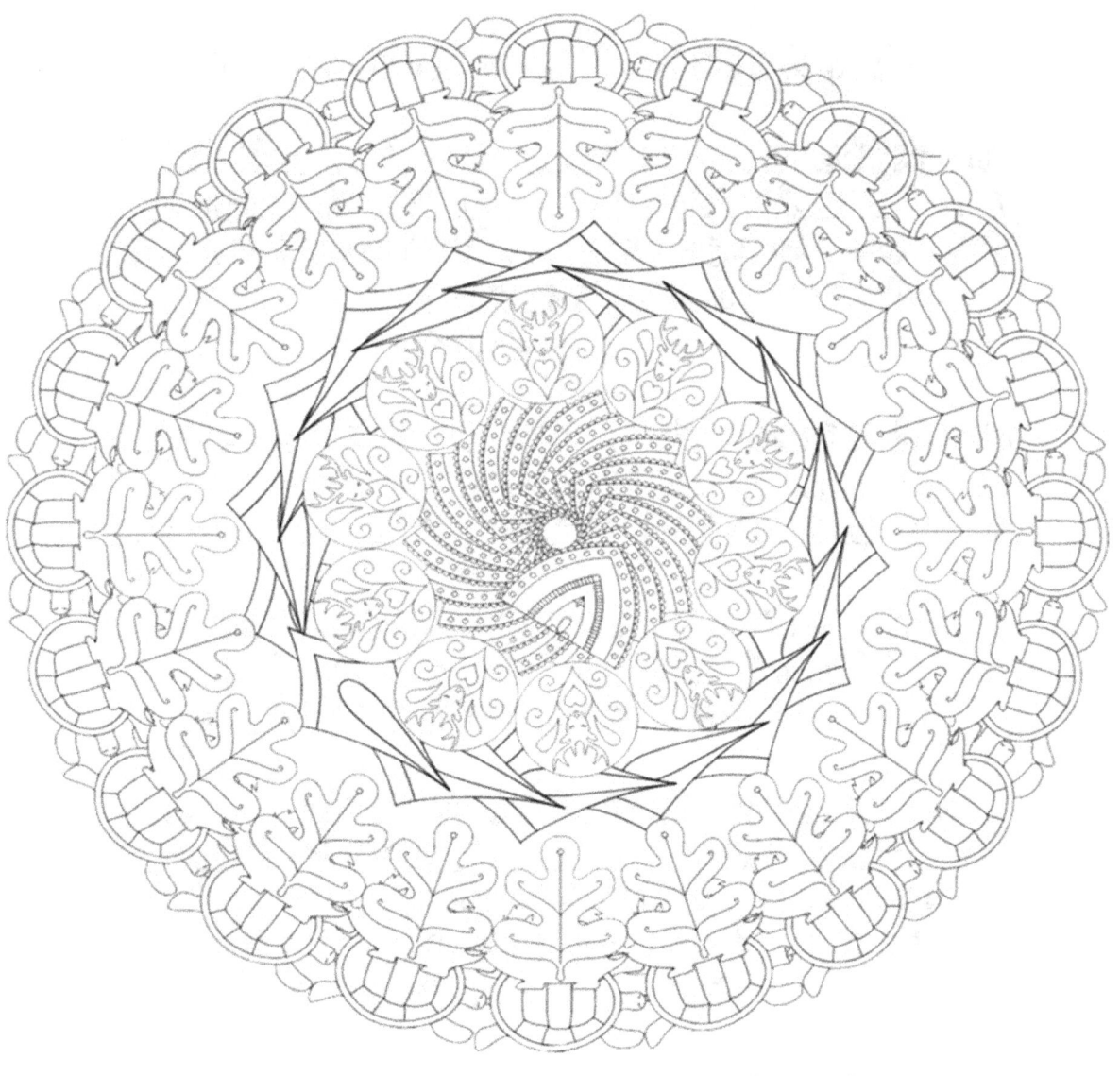

"Let me, O let me bathe my soul
in colors; let me swallow the
sunset and drink the rainbow."
– Kahlil Gibran

A NOTE FROM THE AUTHOR/ARTIST

Thank you so much for purchasing 'And I Color', another Color My Visions® adult coloring book! Your support is allowing me to pursue my dream of being a professional photographer and published author.

I was born and raised in South Carolina, spent 22 years in Chicago and now reside in Florida where I work as a freelance photographer and author.

In my free time I enjoy traveling, yoga, biking, Scrabble, chess and spending time with my children, family and friends.

If you enjoyed this book, please leave a review, then tag and follow @tolenmedia to be informed when the next Color My Visions® coloring book is released and also for details on all my other creative projects.

Your contribution for this work will allow me to devote precious time and resources to the next installment of inspiring quotes and more of my own original coloring pages. The world can always use more inspiration and smiles.

Thanks again for your support!

Love,
Christopher Conrad Tolen

www.ingramcontent.com/pod-product-compliance
Lightning Source LLC
Chambersburg PA
CBHW080527220526
45465CB00006B/2620